Physical Characteristics of the Norwegian Elkhound

(from the American Kennel Club breed standard)

Body: Short and close-coupled with the rib cage accounting for most of its length.

Topline: The back is straight and strong from its high point at the withers to the root of the tail.

Tail: Set high, tightly curled, and carried over the centerline of the back.

Hindquarters: Moderate angulation at stifle and hock. Thighs are broad and well muscled. Feet as in front.

Height: At the withers for dogs is 20.5 inches, for bitches 19.5 inches.

Weight: For dogs about 55 pounds, for bitches about 48 pounds.

Norwegian Elkhound

By Juliette Cunliffe

Contents

KENNEL CLUB BOOKS® **NORWEGIAN ELKHOUND**

ISBN: 1-59378-306-X

308 Main Street, Allenhurst, NJ 07711 USA
Cover Design Patented: US 6,435,559 B2 • Printed in South Korea

10 9 8 7 6 5 4 3 2 1

Photography by Carol Ann Johnson
with additional photographs by:

Mary Bloom, Paulette Braun, Carolina Biological Supply, Isabelle Français, Bill Jonas, Dr. Dennis Kunkel, Tam C. Nguyen, Mr. B. T. & Mrs. E. V. Nichols, Prof. Dr. Robert L. Peiffer, Jr., Phototake and Jean Claude Revy.

Illustrations by Patricia Peters.

The publisher wishes to thank all of the owners whose dogs are featured in this book, including Robert Greaves and Patricia Trotter.

The Norwegian Elkhound breed dates back many thousands of years. The breed can claim to be one of the oldest dog breeds in existence.

HISTORY OF THE NORWEGIAN ELKHOUND

The Norwegian Elkhound is one of the Arctic breeds, all of which have long histories, but the Norwegian Elkhound is said to date back to four or five thousand years before Christ, which by anyone's standards is a very long while! The period to which the breed dates back was discovered as a result of excavations at Jaeren in western Norway. Here a number of skeletons of both men and animals were found, among them four dogs. Professor Brinchmaun pronounced these skeletons to be undoubtedly of Norwegian Elkhound type. Two were almost identical to the Norwegian Elkhound of recent centuries; the other two were smaller, belonging to *Canis palustris*, which is similar to the Norwegian Elkhound.

ELK HUNTING

In Scandinavia the hunting of the elk is something of a social occasion. Hunters are dressed in red caps or vests, an obligatory color, so that they are not shot in error in the dense forests. To hunt elk is demanding for the dogs and the men, both of which need to be in excellent physical condition!

Undoubtedly the Norwegian Elkhound can claim to be one of the oldest breeds in the world. The breed was the companion of Stone Age man, and since then it has been the large-game hunter and watchdog of western Scandinavia. Based on the aforementioned and other evidence, it certainly appears that the Norwegian Elkhound has been established since prehistoric times and has been domesticated since written records began. In Norway's rural districts, the Norwegian Elkhound has long been kept by farmers, hunters and herdsmen. All of them used this dog for outdoor work in a rugged country with harsh climatic conditions.

ELKHOUNDS AND VIKINGS

The "Viking Age" is considered to have commenced in the year 793 AD, and the Norwegian Elkhound was certainly a companion of the Vikings. Norwegian Elkhounds were the first "sea dogs," accompanying their masters on their journeys through Europe and North America.

Viking commanders were buried on land with their ships,

DIFFERENT NAMES

Over time, the Norwegian Elkhound has acquired different names. In Britain the breed is known simply as "Elkhound." In Norway and Sweden it is known as "Norrland Spets," "Grahuynd" and "den Graa Dyrehund," the latter meaning "gray game dog." "Elkhound" is actually a mistranslation of the name "Elghund," which really means "Elk-dog," and there has long been controversy as to whether or not the Norwegian Elkhound is a hound in the truest sense of the word.

and along with their possessions were often their dogs. Indeed, their dogs were fitting companions for their journey into Valhalla, considered heaven by the Vikings. Bas-relief pictures have depicted Norwegian Elkhounds hunting moose, but Viking life came to an end as a result of closer relations with developing Europe and with Christianity. With the decline of the Vikings, the Norwegian Elkhound also suffered, both in quantity and in quality. However, a small number of dogs, albeit seemingly not of particularly high quality, remained scattered about in villages. These were the dogs that played an integral part in preventing the extinction of the breed.

The Norwegian Elkhound was cherished by the Vikings and appears in many of the old Viking sagas. The breed has retained a strong hunting instinct and, in Norway, still cannot compete in conformation classes unless it has earned a hunting certificate.

THE ELKHOUND AT WORK

A versatile dog, the Norwegian Elkhound was used for help in hunting not only elk but also reindeer and bear. Although recognized as one of the spitz breeds, the Norwegian Elkhound finds itself exhibited in the Hound Group at shows. The breed was, though, once known as the Scandinavian Pointer, as it was also used as a gundog for blackcock.

The Norwegian Elkhound is renowned for its power of scent, and under favorable conditions is capable of scenting a bear or an elk as far as three miles' distance. The Norwegian Elkhound could be used as a "Los-hund," meaning "loose dog," or as a "Band-hund," meaning "lead dog." Although generally allowed to range free, he could work at the end of a 20-foot leash, attached to the master's belt.

If unleashed, the dog would quarter the ground, scenting both the ground and the air, and sometimes standing on his hind legs to obtain a better scent. Upon approaching the quarry, the dog would move more slowly and quietly, so as not to startle the animal. The hunter could be

A photo from the 1920s shows British fancier Stuart Thompson with a pack of Norwegian Elkhounds that has encountered the trail of an otter.

several miles distant, so the remarkable Norwegian Elkhound could find himself in the position of having to keep a large and powerful animal at bay for as long as an hour. Such a method of hunting demanded exceptional endurance, courage and intelligence on the part of the hound, not least because the elk would use both feet and antlers to strike at its adversary. It was the Norwegian Elkhound's compact, short-backed build that allowed him to avoid the elk's hooves and antlers, and the Norwegians described the Norwegian Elkhound as being able to bounce in an out of range in the manner of a rubber ball. The quarry was held at bay by means of the hound's barking and dodging, and the Norwegian Elkhound's bell-like voice, gradually increasing in volume, would alert the hunter to the scene, whereupon the quarry could be dispatched.

Until the early years of the 20th century, the Norwegian Elkhound was bred largely for hunting ability, making the hunting instinct still very strong in today's dog. By the 1920s, a restriction had been placed on the number of elk allowed to be killed.

NATIONAL BREED

The Norwegian Elkhound is the national breed of Norway and was also the national breed of Sweden until being replaced by its relative the Jamthund. When the Norwegian Kennel Club held its first show in 1898, the Norwegian Elkhound was selected to appear on the club's medallion.

Stuart Thompson introduces a rat to his excited hounds. Photo circa 1927.

However, the breed was still used for its original purpose at that time, albeit to a modified extent.

THE ELKHOUND AS GUARD

In Norway the Norwegian Elkhound was treated as a hardy animal and was left outside even during the harsh winter months. He was rarely kept kenneled or chained, but was allowed to roam at will, allowing this remarkable dog to protect his master and his master's stock. The Norwegian Elkhound would warn his master of approaching strangers and would drive off any predators. Indeed this was a dog that earned his keep well in Norway.

NINETEENTH-CENTURY BREED REVIVAL

In 1865 the renowned Norwegian hunter and sportsman, Consul Jens Gram of Ask, bred Bamse Gram, believed to be the Norwegian Elkhound to which pedigrees can be traced back the farthest. Breeding from lines back to this hound, the Norwegian Elkhound was revived.

It was in 1877 that the Norwegian Hunters' Association held its first dog show, and, as the years progressed, breeding records and stud books were established. A breed standard having been

Norwegian postage stamps featuring native breeds: (top) the Norwegian Elkhound, (center) the Norwegian Buhund and (bottom) the Norwegian Lundehund.

drawn up, Norwegian breeders began to center their attention on the Norwegian Elkhound. The breed became known as show dogs in addition to their traditional roles as hunters and outdoor workers.

THE NORWEGIAN ELKHOUND IN THE US

The first imports to the United States arrived in 1913. Three dogs named Koik, Bimba and Laila were registered with the American Kennel Club (AKC) by owner Gottlieb Lechner of Idaho. The first decade of activity in the US yielded minimal results, with only 11 dogs being registered and another 12 being imported and registered by the end of the 1920s.

Vindsval kennels, owned by Bayard Boyesen of Winchester, New Hampshire, was established in 1924; it was the first Elkhound kennel to be established in the US. Other kennels from the early period include: Barbara Thayer Hall's Stonewall kennels; A. Wells Peck's Pitch Road kennels; F. Wood and V. Hubbard's Narvikwood kennels; Edith S. Kozak's Bjorn-Lass kennels and L.F. Smith's Stonylea kennels. The year 1925 marked the breed's first entrance into the Westminster Kennel Club show.

Ch. Grimm of Lifjell holds the honor of being the first Norwegian Elkhound to finish his AKC championship. Grimm, a Norwegian import, won the title in 1926. He was owned by Walter Channing of Brixton kennels in Dover, Massachusetts.

THE LEGEND OF THE NORWEGIAN ELKHOUND'S TAIL

There is a charming legend about how the Norwegian Elkhound came to have his distinctively curled tail. The story revolves around a brave hunter and his Norwegian Elkhound, Bram, who was always by his master's side. Following a fight, the owner killed another man and, in consequence, fled into the forest with his dog. They lived together in mountain caves for years and, in the deep snow, Bram's tail frequently became encrusted with ice and snow. This caused the dog's tail to drag behind him like a frozen broom, which made hunting difficult. One day his master decided to tie Bram's tail over the dog's back with a leather thong; since then, the Norwegian Elkhound has always had a curled tail.

Ch. Vin-Melca's Smuggler won 25 Bests in Show for breeder-handler, Pat Craige (Trotter).

NORDIC ANCESTOR

Along with many other Nordic breeds, the Norwegian Elkhound is likely to be descended from the hunting swamp dog, or "Torvmosehund," used by the itinerant peoples of northern Europe. It appears that these dogs were brought to Scandinavia during the tribes' migration.

In 1934, 89 dogs were registered with the AKC, and in the following year 150 were registered. The year 1934 also marked the foundation of the parent club, the Norwegian Elkhound Association of America (NEEA); the AKC approved the new club in 1936. The gentlemen responsible for organizing the club were Bayard Boyesen, David Wooley and Lawrence Lictfield; during its first year of existence, it had 35 members.

Important American Kennels

The most influential long-standing Elkhound kennel in the US is Vin-Melca Elkhounds, owned and operated by breeder/judge Patricia Vincent (Craige). Patricia obtained her first Elkhound in 1949 (at a very young age) from the Joyce Creek kennels in North Carolina, known for their hunting dogs. Her first dog, Ch. Ulf's Madam Helga, was bred to Ch. Carro of Ardmere, owned by Pitch Road kennels, and got her first Vin-Melca dog: Vin-Melca's Carro Again. About ten years later, she bought Vin-Melca's Rebel Rouser ("Vicky") and bred her to the aging Carro Again, yielding Ch. Vin-Melca's Astridina. Patricia was fast on track to creating her ideal Elkhound: a cookie-cutter level of perfection that few breeders in

Ch. Windy Cove Rowdy Ringo, out of Tusko and Tona, produced Ch. Vin-Melca's Howdy Rowdy, a top show dog and sire.

dogs have ever achieved. Astridina, bred to Ch. Crafdal Trigvie Vikingsson, produced Ch. Vin-Melca's Vikina.

Patricia moved to the West Coast in the 1960s, where she met and married Dr. John Craige. It was in Carmel, California where the Vin-Melca dynasty rooted and prospered. Among the great Vin-Melca dogs was Ch. Vin-Melca's Vicksen, whelped in 1964, the sire of three Best in Show (BIS) winners and himself a Best in Show and specialty show winner. His BIS offspring include Ch. Vin-Melca's Vagabond, Valley Forge and Viscount. Following in his uncle Viscount's pawprints, Ch. Vin-Melca's Smuggler won 25 Best in Show awards and was Group Two at Westminster Kennel Club in 1984.

THE ELKHOUND'S SHARE

In Norway, credit was invariably given to the dog rather than to the hunter. It has been said that a dog would refuse to work for a hunter whose shot was poor, nor would a dog work for a hunter who would not give him some of the meat.

Ch. Vin-Melca's Howdy Rowdy, the winner of the 1968 national, became the top-producing sire in the breed, with 166 champions to his name. One of those 166 champions was Ch. Vin-Melca's Harlow, the top-producing bitch of her time, with 25 champions. Another Vin-Melca bitch, Ch. Vin-Melca's Last Call, broke the record with 27 champions; she also had 14 BIS wins.

Ch. Vin-Melca's Last Call, a multiple BIS winner, is the breed's top dam of all time.

Another great BIS dog for Vin-Melca was Ch. Vin-Melca's Vagabond, the winner of 24 BIS awards as well as the Group at Westminster in 1970 and 1971. This feat was repeated by Ch. Vin-Melca's Nimbus, who won the Group at the Garden in 1977 and

Ch. Vin-Melca's Vagabond, one of many Best in Show champions bred by Patricia Trotter.

A historic winner from the 1970s, Ch. Vin-Melca's Nimbus was the top-winning Elkhound of all time until unseated by Calista.

1979 and became the top-winning male Elkhound of all time.

Ch. Vin-Melca's Calista ("Sarah") also won Westminster Groups twice, in 1989 and 1990. She became the top-winning Elkhound of all time, with 66 Best in Show victories. Her daughter, Ch. Vin-Melca's Marketta, repeated mom's Westminster victories in 1994 and 1995 and is the second all-time bitch, playing second fiddle only to her mom. To date, the Elkhound has only won the Group at Westminster 11 times, 10 times by Vin-Melca dogs.

Ch. Vin-Melca's Calista with Pat Craige (Trotter) in the Group ring at Westminster.

The Vin-Melca prefix continues to be associated with top dogs in the breed. In 2003, for example, four of the five top Elkhounds in the US had Vin-Melca prefixes. Pat Craige (now Trotter, after marrying fellow judge Charles Trotter) has owner-handled most of her winners, and when she's not judging Best in Show, she's running around the group ring with a new Vin-Melca superstar, as she was at Westminster in 2005 with Ch. Vin-Melca Bright Image.

Many Vin-Melca dogs became the foundation dogs of other kennels, including the Red Hill kennels of Freeman and Betty Claus and Sirdal kennels of Lee and Diana Korneiliusen, not to mention others that followed.

In the mid-1950s, Joe and Marie Peterson began their Windy Cove kennels from a puppy out of Greenwood kennels of Linda Scott, Ch. Windy's Tusko of Greenwood. Tusko produced three litters for Windy Cove, yielding nine champions. Ch. Windy Coves Sweda, one of Tusko's offspring, produced ten champions and became a top-producing dam. In the mid-1960s Windy Cove kennels moved from Spokane, Washington to Atascadero, California. Imports from the Oftenasen kennels in Norway have added to the success of the Windy Cove Elkhounds. Among some of the wonderful imports were Ch. Windy Cove Tass av Oftenasen (1966), Ch. Windy Cove Mona av Oftenasen and Windy Cove Riiser Guy (1968), Windy Cove Surprise of Vardetoppen (1972), Ch. Windy Cove Ruffen (1974), Ch. Tortasen's Ola of Windy Cove (1978), Windy Cove Silva of Norway and Ch. Windy Cove Gunnar of Norway (1979), Ch. Rasin Kiva (1984) and Ch. Tortasen's Bjonn O'Windy Cove (1993). In all, there are over 200 American champions and over 30 Canadian champions that bear the Windy Cove prefix. The Petersons are proud of their close association with the "hunting Elkhound" type, and their breeding program has yielded spectacular results over its five decades of operation.

Crafdal Elkhounds of Bob and Glenna Crafts were founded in 1955, based on some great Elkhounds, including future superstar Trygvie Vikingsson, Bamsi Haakonsdotter and Yerta of Greenwood. The Crafts weren't dog-show people, but they entered the dog game as few people ever have: from the top. At their first show they entered Tryg, and he won Best in Show over 100 puppies. He went on to sire more than 65 champions, and his grandson was none other than Ch. Vin-Melca's Howdy Rowdy, the top-producing sire of all time. Another great winner for Crafdal was Crafdal Thunder, a BIS winner. Every kennel is only as good as its bitches, and the bitches that led the way for Crafdal include Friochan Rinta, Ch. Yerta of Greenwood, Ch. Crafdal Lillabo Kvinna, Ch. Crafdal Tryg's Vivla and Ch. Crafdal Tryg's Ruki. Over 300 Elkhound champions bear the Crafdal name, and, although Crafdal isn't active any more, their dogs still are found in the pedigrees of many top Elkhounds.

Ch. Crafdal Trugg'n Thor Rollo, one of the best produced by this top kennel.

The Kamgaard Elkhounds of Margaret Mott trace back to a Crafdal bitch purchase in 1963 when Margaret was a young girl. Every Kamgaard champion is related to her foundation bitch, Crafdal Tryglik Tina. Some of the top dogs from this kennel were Ch. Kamgaard Kiss Me Kate CD, Ch. Kamgaard Tryglikk Kristiana, Ch. Kamgaard Keepsake, Ch. Kamgaard Kit N' Kaboodle, Ch. Kamgaard Korniche, Ch. Kamgaard Kermit and Ch. Kamgaard Kount on Me. Kamgaard also imported a number of excellent Elkhounds from A.M. Lovell's Ravenstone kennels in England as well as some from Norway. The Kamgaard dogs have done wonders for the British Elkhounds, as Margaret has exported some of her best dogs to the UK as well as their progeny.

Basing her kennel primarily on Norwegian imports, Mari Misbeek began her Camalot kennels with Ch. Camalot Ruff's Trogan Av Bella and Ch. Camalot Ruff's Tryste Av Bella from Norway in 1974. Tryste produced nine champions for Camalot and became the foundation bitch for the kennel. Among Tryste's champion offspring was Ch. Camalot Tryste's Totally Hot, who proved an outstanding producer. Mari also imported Ch. Camalot Bella's Trykk, who sired 21 champions; OTCh. Camalot's Bella Tigra, the first Elkhound to gain the Obedience Trial Champion title; and Ch. Camalot's Tigger. Ch. Camalot's Rebel Yell also sired 21 champions and became a national specialty winner. The second OTCh. in the breed was Ch. Camalot's Trully Ayla, also owned and shown by Donald and Marilyn Rotier.

Robert and Victoria Lawton began Vikiro kennels in 1976 with their first show Elkhound, Bermarba's Elske Tara, who became the foundation dam. The Lawtons utilized English and Norwegian lines in their program, and in all racked up 30 champions

A GRAY AREA

In Norway the Norwegian Elkhound is actually the Black Elkhound (or *svart elghound*). The breed that Americans call Norwegian Elkhound is known in Norway as the Gray Elkhound (or *gra elghound*). Covered in a shiny black coat that is dense and shiny, the Black breed tends be smaller with a lighter build, similar to another Norwegian hound, the Norwegian Buhund. Historically, the Black has been separately registered since 1903 and is used to hunt moose and bear.

in their first 10 years of operation. Ch. Roundel's Gizmo of Vikiro, the 1988 specialty winner, was one of the stars produced at this kennel. Other stars included Ch. Vikiro Tara's Macho Man and Ch. Camalot Trulle's Belle Star, two top producers, and Ch. Vikiro Ruby's Ghostdancer.

Attentive to his handler and amenable to the judge's examination, the Elkhound is a willing performer and a beautiful sight in the show ring.

National Specialty Winners at a Glance

The history of the Norwegian Elkhound in the US can be viewed through the lens of the Norwegian Elkhound Association of America's national specialty, a show that attracts the very best dogs in the country. Although some excellent breeders do not lay claim to having bred a specialty winner, many of the top breeders and kennels have. Here is a retrospective of some important winners, their breeders and owners over the first four decades of the NEAA.

The first NEAA national specialty was held on April 7 and 8, 1962, judged by Johnny Aarflot from Norway. The winner was Ch. Gladjac Royal Oslo, bred by Armine St. Germaine and owned by Susan D. Phillips. Three years later, the second national was held, this time judged by Gerd Berbom, also from Norway. Arctic Storm of Pomfret, bred by Susan D. Phillips, won Best in Specialty. The owner was Doris Gustafson.

The third, fourth and fifth national specialties were dominated by Patricia V. Craige and her superb Vin-Melca Elkhounds. The third show, held in 1968, was won by Ch. Vin-Melca's Howdy Rowdy, owned by Patricia Craige and bred by Fred and Lois Turner. The fourth national, held in 1972, was won by Vin-Melca's Huck Finn, judged by the very popular Johnny Aarflot. Also bred and owned by Patricia Craige, Ch. Vin-Melca's Happy Hour won the fifth national over a record-breaking entry of 243 Elkhounds in 1974.

The sixth national was held in Washington, DC in the bicentennial year 1976, and Dr. Jesper Hallingby (of Norway) selected E.A. Hillman's Loki of Stormy Lea, bred by Brian and Lynn Riley, as Best in Specialty. At the seventh national, two years later, in 1978, Titanic's Porcupine Pie quilled the top prize over 256 Elkhounds, under Dr. Arthur E.T. Sneeden, the first non-Norwegian to judge a NEAA national. This bitch was bred by Buzz Sodeman and owned by Joel and Nan Tessin.

The 1980s rolled in with Ch. Vin-Melca's Matinee Idol, owned by Pat Craige and Peter Eckroat, winning the eighth national in 1980. Idol was bred by Robert Maddox. The 1982 winner, Karin's Yogi Bear, was bred by Barbara A. Innes and owned by Gary Proudfoot. The tenth national (1984) winner was Windy Cove Chief Cochise, owned and bred by Marie Peterson. Ch. Kirksstead Olav, owned by T. and C. Reese and Robert Ness won the 1986 national. The 1988 show attracted a record entry of 376 dogs, and the Best in Specialty victor was Ch. Roundel's Gizmo of Vikiro, bred by Bonnie Turner and owned by Robert and Victoria Lawton.

Among the winners from the 1990s forward are Ch. Norelka's Surfs Up at Ardon's, Ch. Norelka's Sky Gazer For Trevin, Ch. Bona Jade's Leggs Diamond and Windy Cove Norgren Wild Pride.

ELKHOUNDS IN SCANDINAVIA TODAY

In Norway the Norwegian Elkhound is still treated very much as a working and hunting dog, though the hunting season lasts for only about three weeks in the month of October. Depending upon the population of elk in any given area, a hunter is granted a strict license to kill only a certain number, and this figure is broken down into calves and adults, bulls and cows. In Sweden and Finland the hunting season is open, so many Norwegian hunters cross the borders into neighboring countries after their own short season has closed.

The importance of hunting ability in this breed is clear when one takes into consideration that, in Scandinavia, a Norwegian Elkhound cannot gain the title of Show Champion without receiving a first grade in a Hunting Trial. Dog shows in this breed focus on much more than looks.

MEET THE SWEDISH ELKHOUND

Developed to hunt in the deep snows of its homeland, the Jamthund of Sweden is another elkhound breed that is used to hunt moose. In Sweden there is also a White Elkhound that is a variation of the (Gray) Norwegian Elkhound and the Jamthund. This new breed was recognized in 1993 in its homeland.

CHARACTERISTICS OF THE NORWEGIAN ELKHOUND

WHY THE ELKHOUND?

Undoubtedly every Norwegian Elkhound owner and fancier has been drawn to the breed for a slightly different reason, and it is only fair to say that the Norwegian Elkhound is certainly not the breed for everyone. It is, in all respects, a natural and unspoiled dog; those who would like to own an elegantly presented showpiece or those who are happy to sit at home all day by the fireplace had better look elsewhere!

Having said that, a Norwegian Elkhound without a doubt likes to be treated as part of the family. This is not a kennel dog, this is a dog that needs to live in the home and be part of family life. A Norwegian Elkhound needs lots of attention and should be given meaningful activity to keep his mind active and to keep him out of mischief! As a companion and friend, breed enthusiasts say that the Norwegian Elkhound is second to none. He has a tremendous capacity for affection and, not least, a brilliant brain.

HEART-HEALTHY

In this modern age of ever-improving cardio-care, no doctor or scientist can dispute the advantages of owning a dog to lower a person's risk of heart disease. Studies have proven that petting a dog, walking a dog and grooming a dog all show positive results toward lowering your blood pressure. The simple routine of exercising your dog—going outside with the dog and walking, jogging or playing catch—is heart-healthy in and of itself. If you are normally less active than your physician thinks you should be, adopting a dog may be a smart option to improve your own quality of life as well as that of another creature.

PERSONALITY

The Norwegian Elkhound should be a friendly, intelligent and

NAUGHTY DOG!

Norwegian Elkhounds can, like other dogs, easily get into bad habits if they are allowed to do so. A Norwegian Elkhound "just being naughty" at the age of eight weeks or so may be charming, or even humorous, but an adult dog who is still just as naughty is quite a different matter! Sensible upbringing is therefore essential.

independent dog, one that should display no nervousness. The breed is not generally aggressive by nature; it takes extreme provocation to elicit an aggressive response. However, a Norwegian Elkhound can indeed be protective and can be possessive when it comes to looking after his own family and his family's property.

The Norwegian Elkhound has a sense of dignity and a certain independence of character, with an ability to "size up" his owner or another person very quickly. Elkhounds are typically friendly dogs to all they meet. Further, they quickly can discern which people they should obey and with whom they can get their own way. It is important for a Norwegian Elkhound to be taught exactly who is the leader of your little family pack—and that person should be you!

The Norwegian Elkhound has long been used to hunt the elk (or moose). The elk is a large animal, some might say resembling a horse, that stands around 6 feet tall at the shoulder. The antlers can measure 50–70 inches, and the hooves are extremely powerful. Knowing a little more about the Norwegian Elkhound's quarry tells us something about the character of this remarkable dog.

It should be borne in mind that, in Norway, it was the Elkhounds that led the hunters, not the other way around. This will probably explain something of the way the Norwegian Elkhound behaves when on a leash. The most successful Norwegian Elkhound owners are probably those with strong, confident personalities, those who have the time and energy to train their dogs and take their dogs on long walks.

Norwegian Elkhounds will obey within reason, but under no circumstances will they allow themselves to become slaves. If taught, they realize that they must not touch poultry or sheep, but they also do not expect to be at their masters' beck and call. A Norwegian Elkhound will always be by his master's side, or thereabouts, but must have a reasonable amount of freedom.

It should be mentioned that the Norwegian Elkhound is a vocal breed. Norwegian Elkhounds are very alert dogs and are likely to bark at unexpected noises, or at someone or something they perceive to be an intruder. Coupled with this is the volume of the Norwegian Elkhound's bark. For hunting purposes, it is necessary that the Norwegian Elkhound's voice is able to be heard over miles of mountainous terrain. This translates into a bark that is loud enough to be something of nuisance to neighbors if heard frequently. Owners should remember that Norwegian Elkhounds have a tendency to get bored easily, and bored dogs usually bark. Keeping your Elkhound active in mind and body is tantamount to a happy dog and good relations with neighbors.

THE FASCINATING ELKHOUND

When Kitty Heffer wrote about the Norwegian Elkhound in 1969, she said that she had used the word "fascinating" to describe her first Norwegian Elkhound, and this was the word that applied to all Norwegian Elkhounds she had met since. The dogs were alike in many ways, but each had just that spark of individuality to keep one guessing.

PHYSICAL CHARACTERISTICS

Although not particularly tall, the Norwegian Elkhound is a powerful dog contained in a compact body that is square in outline. The chest is broad and deep, and the short, wide loin has little tuck-up.

Form and function go hand in hand, as a breed's physical characteristics are suited to its task and to the area in which it originated. Many examples of functional physical traits are found in the Norwegian Elkhound.

An interesting gauge by which leg length is compared to overall height is that the distance from the brisket to the ground should not be less than half of the overall height at the withers (highest point of the shoulder). The topline is straight and level.

The straight forelegs have good bone, but this should not be coarse. The hindlegs are firm, strong and powerful, with little but definite bend at the stifles and hocks. In comparison with the size of the dog, the Norwegian Elkhound's feet are fairly small. They are slightly oval in shape, with tightly closed, well-arched toes. There is protective hair between the thick footpads, again reminding us of the terrain and conditions under which this breed works in its homeland.

Head and Ears

The Norwegian Elkhound's skull is wedge-shaped and is comparatively broad between the ears. The foreface is also broad at its root and it tapers evenly, whether seen from above or from the side. It should never be pointed. The bridge of the nose is straight and is about the same length as the forehead. On the head, the skin is tight and should have no wrinkle.

Setting off the head are the Norwegian Elkhound's small, firm, high-set ears. These are erect, pointed and highly mobile, so that, when the dog is alert, the outer edge of the ear is vertical. In shape, they are slightly taller than the width of the base of the ear.

> **GOOD IDEA!**
> Although Norwegian Elkhounds can be obedience trained, they need to be motivated and cannot be trained in the same way as breeds such as the Border Collie. The Norwegian Elkhound has been bred to track down game and to keep it at bay on his own. Because of this, he tends to rely on his own decisions. An Norwegian Elkhound, therefore, needs to think that a training exercise is his own idea!

Tail

The strong tail is set on high, thickly coated and tightly curled, preferably over the center line of the back.

Size

Ideally, dogs should be 20.5 inches in height at the shoulder and should weigh about 55 pounds. Bitches are a little smaller, measuring ideally 19.5 inches high and weighing about 48 pounds.

Movement

The Norwegian Elkhound's movement should reflect the breed's original purpose. Because of the Norwegian Elkhound's work in Scandinavia, it is important that the dog's movement demonstrates both agility and endurance with an even, effortless stride. As speed increases, both front and hind legs converge equally in straight lines toward the center line.

Coat

Like most dogs from the northern regions, the Norwegian Elkhound has a double coat that is close, abundant and weather-resistant. The soft, dense, woolly undercoat is important for insulation against the cold, while the coarse, straight outer coat protects against rain, sleet and snow. On the head and front of the legs, the coat is short and smooth, but is slightly longer on the back of the front legs. It is longest of all on the neck, where it forms a ruff, and also on the back of the thighs and on the tail, which should never be trimmed.

The coat sheds in small amounts throughout the year, but profusely twice annually. During these times, special attention to grooming is an absolute necessity. Those who have a particular dislike to finding dog hairs around the home should probably think twice about owning a Norwegian Elkhound, and most people with allergies would be unwise to own this breed. The Norwegian Elkhound instinctively keeps himself clean and seems to shed dirt and other things trapped in the coat with ease. Therefore, despite their abundant coats, Norwegian Elkhounds do not have "doggy odor."

Feeding too many tidbits can cause skin problems in Norwegian Elkhounds, especially if those seemingly enjoyable snacks contain too much starch. A well-balanced diet will often correct the problem, bringing skin and coat condition back into order.

Color

Norwegian Elkhounds can be found in various shades of gray, with black tips on the outer coat. The coat is lighter on the chest, stomach, legs, underside of tail and buttocks, forming what is known as a "harness mark." The ears and foreface are dark, and a dark line from the eye to the ear is desirable. The Norwegian Elkhound's undercoat is a pure, pale gray. Any white markings, as well as lighter-colored "spectacles" around the eyes, are undesirable, as is a sooty color that can sometimes be found on the lower legs.

Teeth

The Norwegian Elkhound has a typical canine bite with the upper teeth closely overlapping the lower ones in what is known as a scissor bite. Teeth should be set square to the jaws, which should be strong.

HEALTH CONSIDERATIONS

The Norwegian Elkhound is basically a natural, unspoiled dog that does not encounter as many health problems as some other breeds. As time moves on and genetic research progresses further, more and more problems are discovered; this, however, can only be for the future benefit of the breed.

To be forewarned is to be forearmed, so this section is not intended to put fear into those who are considering becoming Norwegian Elkhound owners. Instead, I hope it will help to enlighten them, so that any health problems encountered can be dealt with as early as possible and in the most appropriate manner. Following are some of the more common problems in the breed; for more detailed information and a complete list, visit the health section at www.neaa.net.

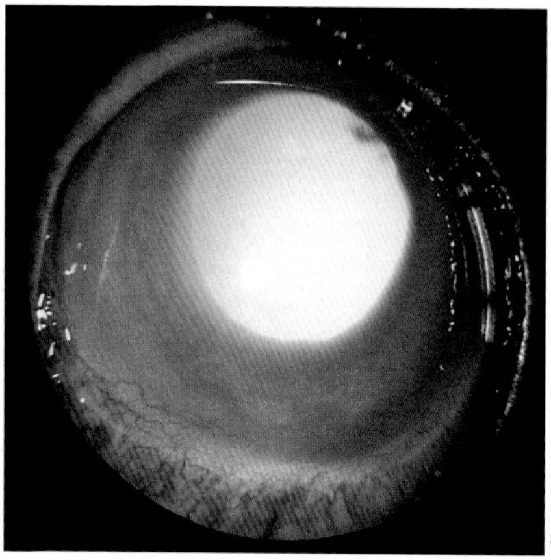

DNA RESEARCH

In the US, a DNA databank is being established for the Norwegian Elkhound, with buccal swabs being donated by Norwegian Elkhound owners and breeders. The NEAA is also sponsoring a breed health survey. These initiatives will allow Norwegian Elkhound breeders to work toward identifying and resolving health problems by genetic screening.

Glaucoma in a dog most commonly occurs as a sudden extreme elevation of intraocular pressure, frequently to three to four times the norm. The eye of this dog demonstrates the common signs of episcleral injection, or redness; mild diffuse corneal cloudiness, due to edema; and a mid-sized fixed pupil.

Photo courtesy of Prof. Dr. Robert L. Peiffer, Jr.

Eye Disease

A prominent hereditary eye disease in the Norwegian Elkhound is progressive retinal atrophy (PRA). The type of PRA found in the Elkhound affects both the rods and the cones, cells that regulate night and day vision, and is called PRCD (progressive rod-cone degeneration). It is inherited as a simple recessive, and major studies are underway to identify the gene that causes this type of PRA in affected breeds. In this way, dogs can be identified as PRA-free, carriers or affected, and selective breeding can eventually eliminate the problem from these breeds. In the meantime, dogs should be examined frequently throughout their lives and certification numbers obtained from the Canine Eye Registration Foundation (CERF).

Other common eye problems found with varying frequency in the Elkhound include cataracts, glaucoma, ectropion, entropion and distichiasis, along with some other less common problems. CERF ophthalmologic exams, as well as specialized genetic testing that is available separately for some eye problems, should be performed on all Elkhounds, particularly breeding stock.

Renal (Kidney) Disease

The Norwegian Elkhound is one of a number of breeds that is sometimes affected by juvenile renal dysplasia (renal cortical hypoplasia) or, more commonly, JRD. Dedicated breeders today are only too pleased to assist in cooperating with researchers so that this disease may be studied in detail. The sad outcome of the disease is that dogs die of kidney failure between the ages of four months and five years. It is possible for a dog to inherit the gene for the disease and pass on the disease to offspring, yet not exhibit the disease.

The first symptom usually observed in an affected dog is an increase in the production of urine coupled with excessive thirst. When the urine is checked, it is found to be extremely dilute, which is indicative of kidney disease. At later stages, a dog may lose his appetite and have muscular weakness, vomiting, diarrhea and foul-smelling breath. Although there is no cure, there are ways, albeit limited, to manage symptoms as the condition worsens.

Fanconi Syndrome

Fanconi syndrome is another kidney problem; in dogs, it is found in most commonly in the Norwegian Elkhound and the Basenji. Affected dogs have a defect in the renal tubule that causes reduced reabsorption of essential nutrients back into the bloodstream. Not only does this cause a deficiency of certain nutrients but can also create an acidic condition in which bone can begin to dissolve, among other effects. Untreated, this disease and its complications can be life-threatening, but it can be managed with blood monitoring and nutrient supplementation.

Sebaceous Cysts

A number of Norwegian Elkhounds suffer from sebaceous cysts. Although the cysts look rather unpleasant, they are harmless. They are slow-growing bumps under the skin and, although they usually appear on the back or neck, can occur anywhere. This type of cyst generally contains dead skin and other skin particles, and can usually be treated by a vet, who will either express its contents or remove it surgically. In rare cases, a cyst may actually be a type of benign skin tumor, which can be successfully removed.

EPILEPSY

The occasional case of epilepsy, sometimes referred to as non-diagnosed fitting, has been reported in Norwegian Elkhounds. The actual term, epilepsy, refers to any condition in which seizures are recurrent. Often there is loss of consciousness, albeit brief, with convulsive muscle activity; there also may be salivation and involuntary defecation and urination. Many dogs suffering from epilepsy can benefit from anticonvulsant therapy.

The Norwegian Elkhound is one of the breeds included in epilepsy research, with participating organizations in the US and Britain. The goal is to discover the genes responsible for epilepsy in dogs so that careful breeding can reduce the incidence of the disease.

The Norwegian Elkhound is a natural, hardy breed that is not predisposed to many of the health problems that affect other breeds.

THYROID PROBLEMS

Hypothyroidism, a hormonal disorder, is found occasionally in the Norwegian Elkhound. There are many signs of hypothyroidism and, because they can be present in any combination, may easily be mistaken for signs of other diseases. Classic signs are obesity, hair loss and lethargy; the latter leads to muscle wasting, which is caused by an inability to take on sufficient exercise. In classic cases the hair loss is bilaterally symmetrical, affecting the same area on both sides of the body, and generally there are no signs of either itching or scratching.

Hypothyroidism is thought to be inherited. Fortunately, the condition can be managed through medication and diet so that affected dogs can lead normal, happy lives.

Do You Know about Hip Dysplasia?

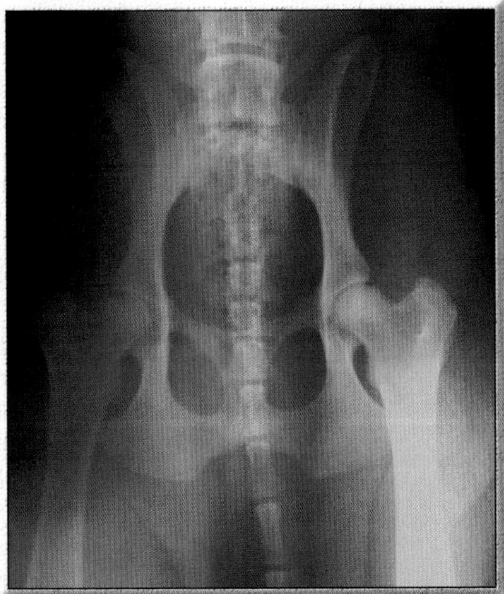

X-ray of a dog with "Good" hips.

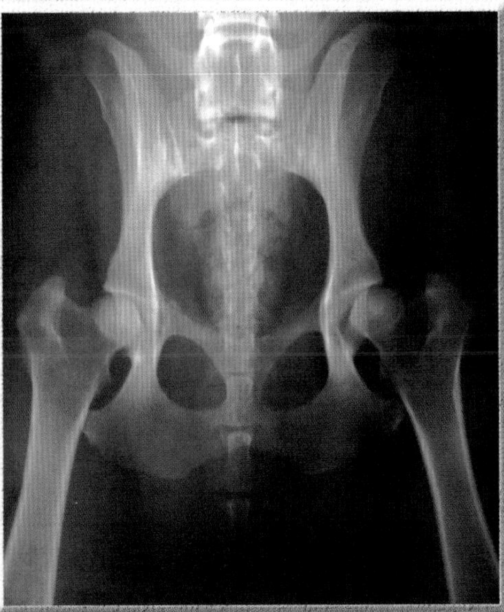

X-ray of a dog with "Moderate" dysplastic hips.

Hip dysplasia is a fairly common condition found in pure-bred dogs. When a dog has hip dysplasia, his hind leg has an incorrectly formed hip joint. By constant use of the hip joint, it becomes more and more loose, wears abnormally and may become arthritic.

Hip dysplasia can only be confirmed with an x-ray, but certain symptoms may indicate a problem. Your dog may have a hip dysplasia problem if he walks in a peculiar manner, hops instead of smoothly runs, uses his hind legs in unison (to keep the pressure off the weak joint), has trouble getting up from a prone position or always sits with both legs together on one side of his body.

As the dog matures, he may adapt well to life with a bad hip, but in a few years arthritis develops and many dogs with hip dysplasia become crippled.

Hip dysplasia is considered an inherited disease and only can be diagnosed definitively by x-ray when the dog is two years old, although symptoms often appear earlier. Some experts claim that a special diet might help your puppy outgrow the bad hip, but the usual treatments are surgical. The removal of the pectineus muscle, the removal of the round part of the femur, reconstructing the pelvis and replacing the hip with an artificial one are all surgical interventions that are expensive, but they are usually very successful. Follow the advice of your veterinarian.

BREED STANDARD FOR THE NORWEGIAN ELKHOUND

INTRODUCTION TO THE BREED STANDARD

The breed standard for the Norwegian Elkhound in the US was set forth by the Norwegian Elkhound Association of America and approved by the American Kennel Club and, like standards for other breeds, can be changed occasionally. Such changes come about from experienced people within the national breed club. It is interesting to look back occasionally at breed standards through the decades and to note some of the alterations that have taken place over time. Those who have an opportunity to research the breed further back may like to read the Norwegian Elkhound breed standard that was published in 1904 in the book *Dogs of All Nations*, compiled by Count Henry Bylandt of the Netherlands. The weight required was "about 60 lbs" which, as readers will see from the present breed standard, which follows, is a bit more than today's requirement. Indeed, there are some other very considerable variances between the standard published in 1904 and that of today: the ears were "of medium size," where now they are "comparatively small;" eye color was specified as "dark brown or yellow-brown," now they are only to be "very dark brown." Undoubtedly the Norwegian Elkhound has a fascinating and absorbing history from many different angles.

All breed standards are designed effectively to paint a picture in words of the ideal representative of a given breed, although each reader will almost certainly have a slightly different way of interpreting these words. After all, when all is said and done, were everyone to interpret a breed's standard in exactly the same way, there would only be one consistent winner within the breed at any given time!

Additionally, reading words alone is never enough to fully comprehend the intricacies of a breed. It is essential also for devotees to watch Norwegian Elkhounds being judged at shows and, if possible, to attend seminars at which the breed is discussed. This enables owners to absorb as much as possible about this highly individual breed of dog. "Hands-on" experience, providing an opportunity to assess the structure of different dogs, is always valuable, especially for those who hope ultimately to judge the breed.

A breed standard is the "blueprint" that undoubtedly helps breeders to produce stock that comes as close as possible to the recognized ideal and helps judges to know exactly what they are looking for in the ring. This enables a judge to make a carefully considered decision when selecting the most typical Norwegian Elkhound present to head his line of winners. However familiar you are with the Norwegian Elkhound, it is always worth refreshing your memory by re-reading the standard, for it is sometimes all too easy to overlook, or perhaps conveniently forget, certain features.

At conformation shows, a dog's success is based on how closely he conforms to the description set forth in an official breed standard. This Norwegian Elkhound had an impressive Hound Group win at England's prestigious Crufts show.

THE AMERICAN KENNEL CLUB STANDARD FOR THE NORWEGIAN ELKHOUND

General Appearance: The Norwegian Elkhound is a hardy gray hunting dog. In appearance, a typical northern dog of medium size and substance, square in profile, close coupled and balanced in proportions. The head is broad with prick ears, and the tail is tightly curled and carried over the back. The distinctive gray coat is dense and smooth lying. As a hunter, the Norwegian Elkhound has the courage, agility and stamina to hold moose and other big game at bay by barking and dodging attack, and the endurance to

Dog in profile; a mature male in full coat with proper substance and correct balance, type and soundness.

track for long hours in all weather over rough and varied terrain.

Size, Proportion, Substance: *Height* at the withers for dogs is 20.5 inches, for bitches 19.5 inches. *Weight* for dogs about 55 pounds, for bitches about 48 pounds. Square in profile and close coupled. Distance from brisket to ground appears to be half the height at the withers. Distance from forechest to rump equals the height at the withers. Bone is substantial, without being coarse.

Head: *Head* broad at the ears, wedge shaped, strong and dry (without loose skin). *Expression* keen, alert, indicating a dog with great courage. *Eyes* very dark brown, medium in size, oval, not protruding. *Ears* set high, firm and erect, yet very mobile. Comparatively small; slightly taller than their width at the base with pointed (not rounded) tips. When the dog is alert, the orifices turn forward and the outer edges are vertical. When relaxed or showing affection, the ears go back, and the dog should not be penalized for doing this during the judge's examination. Viewed from the side, the forehead and back of the *skull* are only slightly arched; the *stop* not large, yet clearly defined. The *muzzle* is thickest at the base and, seen from above or from the side, tapers evenly without being pointed. The bridge of the *nose* is straight, parallel to and about the same length as the skull. *Lips* are tightly closed and *teeth* meet in a scissors bite.

Neck, Topline, Body: *Neck* of medium length, muscular, well set up with a slight arch and with no loose skin on the throat. *Topline*—The back is straight and strong from its high point at the withers to the root of the tail. The *body* is short and close-coupled with the rib cage accounting for most of its length. *Chest* deep and moderately broad; brisket level with points of elbows; and ribs well sprung. *Loin* short and wide with very little tuck-up. *Tail* set high, tightly curled and carried over the centerline of the back. It is thickly and closely haired, without brush. Natural and untrimmed.

Forequarters: Shoulders sloping with elbows closely set on. *Legs* well under body and medium in length; substantial, but not coarse, in bone. Seen from the front, the legs appear straight and parallel. Single dewclaws are normally

FAULTS IN PROFILE

Short neck, extremely upright in shoulders, knuckled over at pasterns, long-backed, low on leg, soft topline, low tail set, poor tail carriage.

Too long in muzzle, lacking correct type and balance, lacking bone, shallow-chested, high on leg, flat feet, ewe-necked, extremely straight behind, sparse coat.

Head study of a mature dog in profile showing proper type, proportion and substance and a pleasing expression.

present. *Feet*—Paws comparatively small, slightly oval with tightly closed toes and thick pads. Pasterns are strong and only slightly bent. Feet turn neither in nor out.

Hindquarters: Moderate angulation at stifle and hock. *Thighs* are broad and well muscled. Seen from behind, legs are straight, strong and without dewclaws. *Feet* as in front.

Coat: Thick, hard, weather resisting and smooth lying; made up of soft, dense, woolly undercoat and coarse, straight covering hairs. Short and even on head, ears and front of legs; longest on back of neck, buttocks and underside of tail. The coat is not altered by trimming, clipping or artificial treatment. Trimming of whiskers is optional. In the show ring, presentation in a natural, unaltered condition is essential.

Color: Gray, medium preferred, variations in shade determined by the length of black tips and

BETTER THAN THE AVERAGE DOG

Even though you may never show your dog, you should still read the breed standard. The breed standard tells you more than just physical specifications such as how tall your dog should be; it also describes how he should act, how he should move and what unique qualities make him the breed that he is. You are not investing money in a pure-bred dog so that you can own a dog that "sort of looks like" the breed you're purchasing. You want a typical, handsome representative of the breed, one that all of your friends and family and people you meet out in public will recognize as the breed you've so carefully selected and researched. If the parents of your prospective puppy bear little or no resemblance to the dog described in the breed standard, you should keep searching!

quantity of guard hairs. Undercoat is clear light silver as are legs, stomach, buttocks and underside of tail. The gray body color is darkest on the saddle, lighter on the chest, mane and distinctive harness mark (a band of longer guard hairs from shoulder to elbow). The muzzle, ears and tail tip are black. The black of the muzzle shades to lighter gray over the forehead and skull. Yellow or brown shading, white patches, indistinct or irregular markings, "sooty" coloring on the lower legs and light circles around the eyes are undesirable. Any overall color other than gray as described above, such as red, brown, solid black, white or other solid color, disqualifies.

Gait: Normal for an active dog constructed for agility and endurance. At a trot the stride is even and effortless; the back remains level. As the speed of the trot increases, front and rear legs converge equally in straight lines toward a center line beneath the body, so that the pads appear to follow in the same tracks (single track). Front and rear quarters are well balanced in angulation and muscular development.

Temperament: In temperament, the Norwegian Elkhound is bold and energetic, an effective guardian yet normally friendly,

FAULTS IN PROFILE

Head coarse and common, ears too large and set wide apart, upright and bullish in shoulders, front feet turned in, soft topline, narrow and straight behind, low tail carriage.

Snipy muzzle, lacking bone and substance, ewe-necked, upright shoulders, narrow front, toes out in front, high in rear, narrow behind, lacking angulation, cow-hocked, flat feet.

MEETING THE IDEAL

The American Kennel Club defines a standard as: "A description of the ideal dog of each recognized breed, to serve as an ideal against which dogs are judged at shows." This "blueprint" is drawn up by the breed's recognized parent club, approved by a majority of its membership and then submitted to the AKC for approval. Standards in different countries are handled differently; for example, in England, all standards and changes are controlled by The Kennel Club.

The AKC states that "An understanding of any breed must begin with its standard. This applies to all dogs, not just those intended for showing." The picture that the standard draws of the dog's type, gait, temperament and structure is the guiding image used by breeders as they plan their programs.

with great dignity and independence of character.

Summary: The Norwegian Elkhound is a square and athletic member of the northern dog family. His unique coloring, weather resistant coat and stable disposition make him an ideal multipurpose dog at work or at play.

Disqualifications: *An overall color other than gray.*

Approved December 13, 1988
Effective February 1, 1989

As the judge reviews the line of dogs, her aim should be to compare each one to the breed standard, not to the other dogs in the ring.

NORWEGIAN ELKHOUND

WHERE TO BEGIN?

Before reaching the decision that you will definitely look for an Norwegian Elkhound puppy, it is essential that you are certain that the Norwegian Elkhound is the most suitable breed for you and your family. If you have carefully researched the breed before making your decision, which of course you should have, you should realize that the Norwegian Elkhound is a rather special breed, a demanding one in many ways. All pros and cons must be carefully weighed against each other before reaching the important decision that an Norwegian Elkhound should join you and your family in your daily life for many years to come.

COST OF OWNERSHIP

The purchase price of your puppy is merely the first expense in the typical dog budget. Quality dog food, veterinary care (sickness and health maintenance), dog supplies and grooming costs will add up to big bucks every year. Can you adequately afford to support a canine addition to the family?

Watching littermates interact is as informative as it is enjoyable. Much can be learned about each pup's personality by observing behavior within the puppy "pack."

Once you have made that decision, you must also ask yourself why you want an Norwegian Elkhound—do you want a pet dog, a show dog, a dog to compete in sporting pursuits? This should be made clear to the breeder when you make your initial inquiries, for you will certainly need to take the breeder's advice as to which available puppy shows the most promise for the show ring (or working, etc.). If you are looking for a pet, you should discuss your family situation with the breeder and, again, take his advice as to which puppy is likely to suit your lifestyle best.

When you have your first opportunity to visit a suitable Elkhound litter, watch the

FINDING A QUALIFIED BREEDER

Before you begin your puppy search, ask for references from your veterinarian, other breeders and other owners to refer you to someone they believe is reputable. Responsible breeders usually raise only one or two breeds of dog. Avoid any breeder who has several different breeds or has several litters at the same time. Dedicated breeders are usually involved with a breed or other dog club. Many participate in some sport or activity related to their breed. Just as you want to be assured of the breeder's qualifications, the breeder wants to be assured that you will make a worthy owner. Expect the breeder to interview you, asking questions about your goals for the pup, your experience with dogs and what kind of home you will provide.

puppies interact together. You will find that different puppies have different personalities, and some will be more boisterous and extroverted than others. You should expect the puppies to come to you, even if they don't know you, so don't take pity on the unduly shy puppy that sits quietly in a corner. Although you will certainly have opinions about which pups appeal to you most, don't forget to take the breeder's advice into careful consideration, as he has the benefit of plenty of firsthand breed knowledge and experience behind his suggestions.

In addition to doing plenty of background "homework" on the breed, you also should have visited a few breed club shows or all-breed shows where the Elkhound has classes, giving you an opportunity to see the breed in some numbers. Shows give you a chance to see the dogs with their breeders and owners, and the opportunity to speak with some people involved in the breed. Be considerate and wait to approach the Elkhound people until after they are finished showing.

Remember that the dog you select should remain with you for the duration of his life, which will hopefully be around 12 years, so making the right decision from the outset is of utmost importance. No dog should be moved from one home to another simply because the owners were not considerate enough to have done sufficient research before selecting the breed. It is always important to remember that, when looking for a puppy, a good breeder will be assessing you as a prospective new owner just as carefully as you are selecting the breeder.

Puppies almost invariably look enchanting, but you must select one from a caring breeder who has given the puppies all the attention they deserve and who has looked after them well. The puppy you select should look well fed, but not pot-bellied, as this might indicate worms. Eyes should look bright and clear, without discharge. The nose should be moist, which is an indication of good health, but it should never be runny. It goes without saying that there should certainly be no evidence of loose stools or parasites. The puppy you choose should have a healthy-looking coat; this is an important indication of good overall health internally. Always check the bite of your selected puppy to be sure that it is neither overshot nor undershot. This may not be too noticeable on a young puppy, but will become more evident as the puppy gets older. A good breeder can advise you on how the bite should mature.

The sex may play a role in your decision when selecting a Norwegian Elkhound puppy. Do you want a male or a female? Males are larger than females, have thicker ruffs and can tend to be more boisterous than their female counterparts. Something else to consider is whether or not to take out veterinary insurance. Vet's bills can mount up, and you must always be certain that sufficient funds are available to give your dog necessary veterinary attention. A good insurance

PEDIGREE VS. REGISTRATION CERTIFICATE

Too often new owners are confused between these two important documents. Your puppy's pedigree, essentially a family tree, is a written record of a dog's genealogy of three generations or more. The pedigree will show you the names as well as performance titles of all dogs in your pup's background. Your breeder must provide you with a registration application, with his part properly filled out. You must complete the application and send it to the AKC with the proper fee. Every puppy must come from a litter that has been AKC-registered by the breeder, born in the US and from a sire and dam that are also registered with the AKC.

The seller must provide you with complete records to identify the puppy. The AKC requires that the seller provide the buyer with the following: breed; sex, color and markings; date of birth; litter number (when available); names and registration numbers of the parents; breeder's name; and date sold or delivered.

policy can certainly help and is best to begin in puppyhood *before* any problems develop.

SELECTING A BREEDER AND PUPPY

If you are convinced that the Norwegian Elkhound is the ideal dog for you, it's time to learn about where to find a puppy and what to look for. You should inquire about breeders in your area who enjoy a good reputation in the breed. You are looking for an established breeder with outstanding dog ethics and a strong commitment to the breed. Where to find such a breeder? The best source for breeder referrals is the national club, the Norwegian Elkhound Association of America (www.neaa.net).

New owners should have as many questions as they have doubts. An established breeder is indeed the one to answer your four million questions and make you comfortable with your choice of the Norwegian Elkhound. An established breeder will sell you a puppy at a fair price if, and only if, the breeder determines that you are a suitable, worthy owner of his dogs. An established breeder can be relied upon for advice, no matter when you need it and no matter how long you have owned the dog. Many breeders maintain relationships with owners of their dogs for the lives of the dogs. A reputable breeder will take a dog back if for some extenuating reason you can no longer keep the dog, which we hope will not be the case.

When choosing a breeder, reputation is much more important than convenience of location. Quality breeders are quiet and unassuming. You hear about them at dog shows and by word

THE FAMILY TREE

Your puppy's pedigree is his family tree. Just as a child may resemble his parents and grandparents, so too will a puppy reflect the qualities, good and bad, of his ancestors, especially those in the first two generations. Therefore it's important to know as much as possible about a puppy's immediate relatives. Reputable and experienced breeders should be able to explain the pedigree and why they chose to breed from the particular dogs they used.

of mouth. You may be well advised to avoid the novice breeder. The novice breeder, trying so hard to get rid of that first litter of puppies, is more than accommodating and anxious to sell you one. That breeder will charge you as much as any established breeder. The novice breeder isn't going to interrogate you and your family about your intentions with the puppy, the environment and training you can provide, etc. That breeder will be nowhere to be found when you need help with your poorly bred, badly adjusted four-pawed monster.

You can see that choosing a breeder is an important first step in dog ownership. Fortunately, the majority of Norwegian Elkhound breeders is devoted to the breed and its well-being. Once you have contacted and met a breeder or two and made your choice about which breeder is best suited to your needs, it's time to visit the litter. Keep in mind that many top breeders have waiting lists. Sometimes new owners have to wait a year or longer for a puppy. If you are really committed to the breeder whom you've selected, then you will wait (and hope for an early arrival!). If not, you may have to go with your second- or third-choice breeder. Don't be too anxious, however. If the breeder doesn't have a waiting list, or any customers, there is probably a good reason!

SIGNS OF A HEALTHY PUPPY

Healthy puppies are robust little fellows who are alert and active, sporting shiny coats and supple skin. They should not appear lethargic, bloated or pot-bellied, nor should they have flaky skin or runny or crusted eyes or noses. Their stools should be firm and well formed, with no evidence of blood or mucus.

Since you are likely to be choosing a Norwegian Elkhound as a pet dog and not a show dog, you simply should select a pup that is friendly, attractive and healthy. Norwegian Elkhounds litters average about six puppies, so you will have a good selection once you have located a desirable

A SHOW PUPPY

If you plan to show your puppy, you must first deal with a reputable breeder who shows his dogs and has had some success in the conformation ring. The puppy's pedigree should include one or more champions in the first and second generation. You should be familiar with the breed and breed standard so you can know what qualities to look for in your puppy. The breeder's observations and recommendations also are invaluable aids in selecting your future champion. If you consider an older puppy, be sure that the puppy has been properly socialized with people and not isolated in a kennel without substantial daily human contact.

litter. Breeders commonly allow visitors to see their litters by around the fifth or sixth week, and puppies leave for their new homes between the eighth and tenth week. Breeders who permit their puppies to leave early are more interested in a profit than in their puppies' well-being. Puppies need to learn the rules of the pack from their dams, and most dams continue teaching the pups manners and dos and don'ts until at least the eighth week. Breeders spend significant amounts of time with the Norwegian Elkhound toddlers so that the pups are able to interact with the "other species," i.e., humans. Given the long history that dogs and humans have, bonding between the two species is natural but must be nurtured. A well-bred, well-socialized Norwegian Elkhound pup wants nothing more than to be near you and please you.

A COMMITTED NEW OWNER

By now you should understand what makes the Norwegian Elkhound a most unique and special dog, one that may fit nicely into your family and lifestyle. If you have researched breeders, you should be able to recognize a knowledgeable and responsible Norwegian Elkhound breeder who cares not only about his pups but also about what kind of owner you will be. If you have completed the final step in your new journey, you have found a litter, or possibly two, of quality Norwegian Elkhound pups.

A visit with the puppies and their breeder will be an education in itself. Breed research, breeder selection and puppy visitation are very important aspects of finding the puppy of your dreams. Beyond that, these things also lay the foundation for a successful future with your pup. By spending time with the puppies, you will be able to recognize certain behaviors and what these behaviors indicate about each pup's temperament. Which type of pup will complement your family dynamics is best determined by observing the puppies in action within their "pack." Remember that your breeder's expertise and recommendations are so valuable.

GETTING ACQUAINTED
When visiting a litter, ask the breeder for suggestions on how best to interact with the puppies. If possible, get right into the middle of the pack and sit down with them. Observe which pups climb into your lap and which ones shy away. Toss a toy for them to chase and bring back to you. It's easy to fall in love with the puppy who picks you, but keep your future objectives in mind before you make your final decision.

Equally as important as playing and exploring to puppies is napping. It's tiring being a growing pup, and youngsters need plenty of rest.

Although you may fall in love with a bold and brassy male, the breeder may suggest that another pup would be best for you. The breeder's experience in rearing Norwegian Elkhound pups and matching their temperaments with appropriate humans offers the best assurance that your pup will meet your needs and expectations. The type of puppy that you select is just as important as your decision that the Norwegian Elkhound is the breed for you.

The decision to live with any dog is a serious commitment and not one to be taken lightly. Your Elkhound puppy is a living sentient being that will be dependent on you for basic survival for his entire life. Beyond the basics of survival—food, water, shelter and protection—he needs much, much more. The new pup needs love, nurturing and a proper canine education to mold him into a responsible, well-behaved canine citizen. Your Norwegian Elkhound's health and good manners will need consistent monitoring and regular "tune-ups," so your job as a responsible dog owner will be ongoing throughout every stage of his life. If you are not prepared to accept these responsibilities and commit to them for at least the next decade, likely longer, then you are not prepared to own a dog of any breed.

Although the responsibilities of owning a dog may at times tax your patience, the joy of living with your Norwegian Elkhound far outweighs the workload, and a well-mannered adult dog is worth your time and effort. Before your very eyes, your new charge will grow up to be your most loyal friend, devoted to you unconditionally.

Every Norwegian Elkhound pup is a fluffy ball of fun, curiosity and just a touch of mischief.

Once started on solid food, puppies often share "family-style" meals.

YOUR NORWEGIAN ELKHOUND SHOPPING LIST

Just as expectant parents prepare a nursery for their baby, so should you ready your home for the arrival of your Norwegian Elkhound pup. If you have the necessary puppy supplies purchased and in place before he comes home, it will ease the puppy's transition from the warmth and familiarity of his mom and littermates to the brand-new environment of his new home and human family. You will be too busy to stock up and prepare your house after your pup comes home, that's for sure! Imagine how a pup must feel upon being transported to a strange new place. It's up to you to comfort him and to let your little pup know that he is going to be happy with you!

FOOD AND WATER BOWLS

Your puppy will need separate bowls for his food and water.

Stainless steel bowls are generally preferred over plastic bowls since they sterilize better and pups are less inclined to chew on the metal. Heavy-duty ceramic bowls are popular, but consider how often you will have to pick up those heavy bowls! Buy adult-sized pans, as your puppy will grow into them quickly.

The Dog Crate

If you think that crates are tools of punishment and confinement for when a dog has misbehaved, think again. More Norwegian Elkhound breeders are realizing that the crate is the preferred house-training aid as well as for all-around puppy training and safety. Because dogs are natural den creatures that prefer cave-like environments, the benefits of crate use are many. A Norwegian Elkhound should not be crated for long periods and the extent to which you use the crate past house-training will depend on your individual dog and situation, but the crate provides the puppy with his very own "safe house," a cozy place to sleep, take a break or seek comfort with a favorite toy; a travel aid to house your dog when on the road, at motels or at the vet's office; a training aid to help teach your puppy proper toileting habits; a place of solitude when non-dog people happen to

The three most common crate types: mesh on the left, wire on the right and fiberglass on top.

SELECTING FROM THE LITTER

Before you visit a litter of puppies, promise yourself that you won't fall for the first pretty face you see! Decide on your goals for your puppy—show prospect, hunting dog, obedience competitor, family companion—and then look for a puppy who displays the appropriate qualities. In most litters, there is an alpha pup (the bossy puppy), and occasionally a shy fellow who is less confident, with the rest of the litter falling somewhere in the middle. "Middle-of-the-roaders" are safe bets for most families and novice competitors.

Your most important initial purchase for your Norwegian Elkhound may well be his crate. Get a sturdy crate, large enough for a fully-grown dog; the crate should last for your dog's lifetime.

drop by and don't want a lively puppy—or even a well-behaved adult dog—saying hello or begging for attention.

Crates come in several types, although the wire crate and the fiberglass airline-type crate are the most popular. Both are safe and your puppy will adjust to either one, so the choice is up to you. The wire crates offer better visibility for the pup as well as better ventilation. Many of the wire crates easily fold into suitcase-size carriers. The fiberglass crates, similar to those used by the airlines for animal transport, are sturdier and more den-like. However, the fiberglass crates do not fold down and are less ventilated than wire crates; this can be problematic in hot weather. Some of the newer crates are made of heavy plastic mesh; they are very lightweight and fold into slim-line suitcases. However, a mesh crate might not be suitable for a pup with manic chewing habits.

Don't bother with a puppy-sized crate. Although your Norwegian Elkhound will be a wee fellow when you bring him home, he will grow up in the blink of an eye and your puppy crate will be useless. Purchase a crate that will accommodate an adult Norwegian Elkhound. A crate of about 36–42 inches long by 24–26 inches wide by 28 inches high should fit him nicely.

CRATE EXPECTATIONS

To make the crate more inviting to your puppy, you can offer his first meal or two inside the crate, always keeping the crate door open so that he does not feel confined. Keep a favorite sturdy toy or two in the crate for him to play with. You can also cover the crate at night with a lightweight sheet to make it more den-like and remove the stimuli of household activity. Never put him into his crate as punishment or as you are scolding him, since he will then associate his crate with negative situations and avoid going there.

Bedding and Crate Pads

Your puppy will enjoy some type of soft bedding in his "room" (the crate), something he can snuggle into to feel cozy and secure. Old towels or blankets are good choices for a young pup, since he may (and probably will) have a toileting accident or two in the crate or decide to chew on the bedding material. Once he is fully trained and out of the early chewing stage, you can replace the puppy bedding with a permanent crate pad if you prefer. Crate pads and other dog beds run the gamut from inexpensive to high-end doggie-designer styles, but don't splurge on the good stuff until you are sure that your puppy is reliable and won't tear it up or make a mess on it.

Puppy Toys

Just as infants and older children require objects to stimulate their minds and bodies, puppies need toys to entertain their curious brains, wiggly paws and achy teeth. A fun array of safe doggie toys will help satisfy your puppy's chewing instincts and distract him from gnawing on the leg of your antique chair or your new leather sofa. Most puppy toys are cute and look as if they would be a lot of fun, but not all are necessarily safe or good for your puppy, so use caution when you go puppy-toy shopping.

Puppies often become attached to a favorite toy that they like to carry around.

Norwegian Elkhounds do chew, especially if bored, and only the hardest, strongest toys should be offered to them. The best "chewcifiers" are nylon and hard rubber bones, which are safe to gnaw on and come in sizes appropriate for all age groups and breeds. The provision of safe chews and marrow bones gives a Norwegian Elkhound much enjoyment. However, bones and chews must be very carefully selected so that they do not splinter, and should always be disposed of when they show any sign of becoming dangerous. Be especially careful of natural bones, which can splinter or develop dangerous sharp edges; pups can easily swallow or choke on those bone splinters. Veterinarians often tell of surgical nightmares involving bits of splintered bone, because in addition to the danger of choking, the sharp pieces can damage the intestinal tract.

Sharing a chew and keeping up on current events, these pups are happily occupied.

Similarly, rawhide chews, while a favorite of most dogs and puppies, can be equally dangerous. Pieces of rawhide are easily swallowed after they get soft and gummy from chewing, and dogs have been known to choke on large pieces of ingested rawhide. Rawhide chews should be offered only when you can supervise the puppy.

Soft woolly toys are special puppy favorites. They come in a wide variety of cute shapes and sizes; some look like little stuffed animals. Puppies love to shake them up and toss them about, or simply carry them around. Be careful of fuzzy toys that have button eyes or noses that your pup could chew off and swallow, and make sure that he does not disembowel a squeaky toy to remove the squeaker! Braided rope toys are similar in that they are fun to chew and toss around, but they shred easily and the strings are easy to swallow. The strings are not digestible and, if the puppy doesn't pass them in his stool, he could end up at the vet's office. As with rawhides, your puppy should be closely monitored with rope toys.

If you believe that your pup has ingested a piece of one of his toys, check his stools for the next couple of days to see if he passes the item when he defecates. At the same time, also watch for signs of intestinal distress. A call to your veterinarian might be in order to get his advice and be on the safe side.

An all-time favorite toy for puppies (young and old!) is the empty gallon milk jug. Hard plastic juice containers—46 ounces or more—are also excellent. Such containers make lots of noise when they are batted about, and

CONFINEMENT

It is wise to keep your puppy confined to a small "puppy-proofed" area of the house for his first few weeks at home. Gate or block off a space near the door he will use for outdoor potty trips. Expandable baby gates are useful to create puppy's designated area. If he is allowed to roam through the entire house or even only several rooms, it will be more difficult to house-train him.

puppies go crazy with delight as they play with them. However, they don't last very long, so be sure to remove and replace them when they get chewed up.

A word of caution about homemade toys: be careful with your choices of non-traditional play objects. Never use old shoes or socks, since a puppy cannot distinguish between the old ones on which he's allowed to chew and the new ones in your closet that are strictly off limits. That principle applies to anything that resembles something that you don't want your puppy to chew.

Collars

A lightweight nylon collar is the best choice for a very young pup. Quick-click collars are easy to put on and remove, and they can be adjusted as the puppy grows. Introduce him to his collar as soon as he comes home to get him accustomed to wearing it. He'll get used to it quickly and won't mind a bit. Make sure that it is snug enough that it won't slip off, yet loose enough to be comfortable for the pup, taking into consideration the abundant neck ruff. You should be able to slip two fingers between the collar and his neck. Check the collar often, as puppies grow in spurts, and his collar can become too tight almost overnight. Rolled collars, rather than flat, are recommended for the Elkhound.

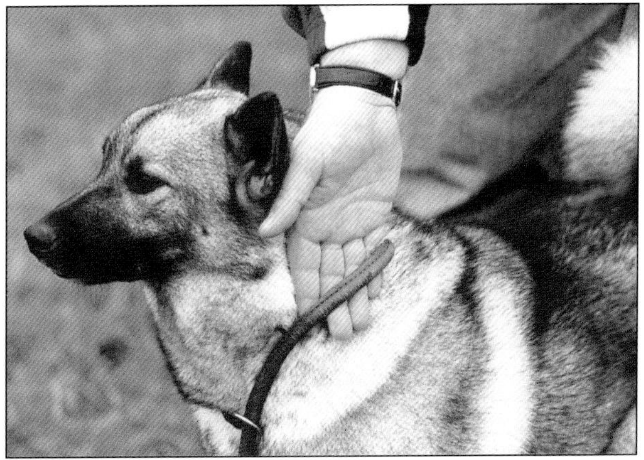

The roll collar is the correct type of leather collar to be used on a Norwegian Elkhound.

Leashes

A 6-foot nylon lead is an excellent choice for a young puppy. It is lightweight and not as tempting to chew as a leather lead. You can switch to a 6-foot leather lead after your pup has grown and is used to walking politely on a lead. For initial puppy walks and house-training purposes, you should invest in a shorter lead so that you have more control over the puppy. At first, you don't want him

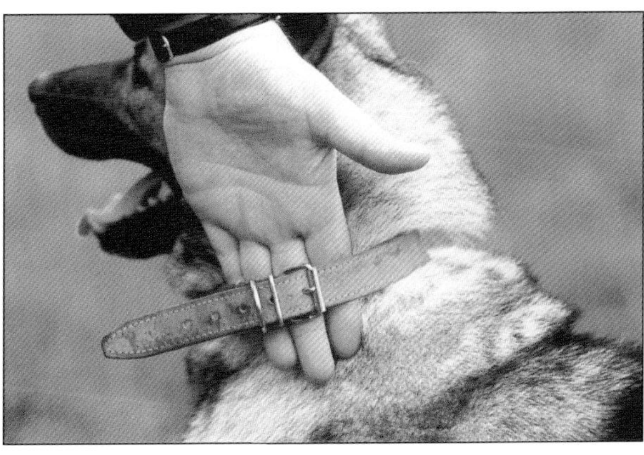

A flat collar like this should NOT be used on a Norwegian Elkhound, as it will damage the coat around the neck.

A Norwegian Elkhound puppy on the move! All pups are curious, even more so those with hunting instincts, so keeping your Norwegian Elkhound supervised and secure is of utmost importance.

wandering too far away from you, and when taking him out for toileting you will want to keep him in the specific area chosen for his potty spot.

Once the puppy is heel-trained with a traditional leash, you can consider purchasing a retractable lead. A retractable lead is excellent for walking adult dogs that are already leash-wise. This type of lead allows the dog to roam farther away from you and explore a wider area when out walking, and also retracts when you need to keep him close to you.

HOME SAFETY FOR YOUR PUPPY

The importance of puppy-proofing cannot be overstated. In addition to making your house comfortable for your Norwegian Elkhound's arrival, you also must make sure that your house is safe for your puppy before you bring him home. There are countless hazards in the owner's personal living environment that a pup can sniff, chew, swallow or destroy. Many are obvious; others are not. Do a thorough advance house check to remove or rearrange those things that could hurt your puppy, keeping any potentially dangerous items out of areas to which he will have access.

Electrical cords are especially dangerous, since puppies view them as irresistible chew toys. Unplug and remove all exposed cords or fasten them beneath baseboards where the puppy cannot reach them. Veterinarians and firefighters can tell you horror stories about electrical burns and house fires that resulted from chewed electrical cords. Consider this a most serious precaution for your Elkhound and the rest of your family.

CREATE A SCHEDULE

Puppies thrive on sameness and routine. Offer meals at the same time each day, take him out at regular times for potty trips and do the same for play periods and outdoor activity. Make note of when your puppy naps and when he is most lively and energetic, and try to plan his day around those times. Once he is house-trained and more predictable in his habits, he will be better able to tolerate changes in his schedule.

Scout your home for tiny objects that might be seen at a pup's eye level. Keep medication bottles and cleaning supplies well out of reach, and do the same with waste baskets and other trash containers. It goes without saying that you should not use rodent poison or other toxic chemicals in any puppy area and that you must keep such containers safely locked up. You will be amazed at how many places a curious puppy can discover!

Once your house has cleared inspection, check your yard. A sturdy fence, embedded at least a foot deep into the ground, will give your dog a safe place to play and potty. Elkhounds are definitely diggers, and they can also jump and climb. A fence of at least 6 feet high will be necessary to contain an agile youngster or adult. Check the fence periodically for necessary repairs. If there is a weak link or space to squeeze through, you can be sure a determined Norwegian Elkhound will discover it.

The garage and shed can be hazardous places, as things like fertilizers, chemicals and tools are usually kept there. It's best to keep these areas off limits to the dog. Antifreeze is especially dangerous to dogs, as they find the taste appealing and it takes only a few licks from the driveway to kill a dog, puppy or adult, small breed or large.

TOXIC PLANTS

Plants are natural puppy magnets, but many can be harmful, even fatal, if ingested by a puppy or adult dog. Scout your yard and home interior and remove any plants, bushes or flowers that could be even mildly dangerous. It could save your puppy's life. You can obtain a complete list of toxic plants from your veterinarian, at the public library or by looking online.

VISITING THE VETERINARIAN

A good veterinarian is your Norwegian Elkhound puppy's best health-insurance policy. If you do not already have a vet, ask friends and experienced dog people in your area for recommendations so that you can select a vet, preferably one experienced in spitz breeds, before you bring your Norwegian Elkhound puppy

"Who, me?" Just look at the sweet face of an Elkhound pup and you'd never believe that he's capable of getting into trouble.

home. Also arrange for your puppy's first veterinary examination beforehand, since many vets do not have appointments immediately available, and your puppy should visit the vet within a day or so of coming home.

It's important to make sure that your puppy's first visit to the vet is a pleasant and positive one. The vet should take great care to befriend the pup and handle him gently to make their first meeting a positive experience. The vet will give the pup a thorough physical examination and set up a schedule for vaccinations and other necessary wellness visits. Be sure to show your vet any health and inoculation records, which you should have received from your breeder. Your vet is a great source of canine health information, so be sure to ask questions and take notes. Creating a health journal for your puppy will make a handy reference for his wellness and any future health problems that may arise.

MEETING THE FAMILY

Your Norwegian Elkhound's homecoming is an exciting time for all members of the family, and it's only natural that everyone will be eager to meet him, pet him and play with him. However, for the puppy's sake, it's best to make these initial family meetings as uneventful as possible so that the pup is not overwhelmed with too much too soon. Remember, he has just left his dam and his littermates and is away from the

KEEP OUT OF REACH

Most dogs don't browse around your medicine cabinet, but accidents do happen! The drug acetaminophen, the active ingredient in certain popular over-the-counter pain relievers, can be deadly to dogs and cats if ingested in large quantities. Acetaminophen toxicity, caused by the dog's swallowing 15 to 20 tablets, can be manifested in abdominal pains within a day or two of ingestion, as well as liver damage. If you suspect your dog has swiped a bottle of medication, get the dog to the vet immediately so that the vet can induce vomiting and cleanse the dog's stomach.

breeder's home for the first time. Despite his fuzzy wagging tail, he is still apprehensive and wondering where he is and who all these strange humans are. It's best to let him explore on his own and meet the family members as he feels comfortable. Let him investigate all the new smells, sights and sounds at his own pace. Children should be especially careful to not get overly excited, use loud voices or hug the pup too tightly. Be calm, gentle and affectionate, and be ready to comfort him if he appears frightened or uneasy.

Be sure to show your puppy his new crate during this first day home. Toss a treat or two inside the crate; if he associates the crate with food, he will associate the crate with good things. If he is comfortable with the crate, you can offer him his first meal inside it. Leave the door ajar so he can wander in and out as he chooses.

FIRST NIGHT IN HIS NEW HOME

So much has happened in your Norwegian Elkhound puppy's first day away from the breeder. He's had his first car ride to his new home. He's met his new human family and perhaps the other family pets. He has explored his new house and yard, at least those places where he is to be allowed during his first weeks at home. He may have visited his new veterinarian. He has eaten his first meal or two away from his dam and littermates. Surely that's enough to tire out an eight-week-old Norwegian Elkhound pup…or so you hope!

It's bedtime. During the day, the pup investigated his crate, which is his new den and sleeping space, so it is not entirely

Chewing, playing, running, making mischief...a puppy has a busy schedule! Believe it or not, your pup will rest almost as much as he's on the go.

PUPPY PARASITES

Parasites are nasty little critters that live in or on your dog or puppy. Most puppies are born with ascarid roundworms, which are acquired from dormant ascarids residing in the dam. Other parasites can be acquired through contact with infected fecal matter. Take a stool sample to your vet for testing. He will prescribe a safe wormer to treat any parasites found in your puppy's stool. Always have a fecal test performed at your puppy's annual veterinary exam.

strange to him. Line the crate with a soft towel or blanket that he can snuggle into and gently place him into the crate for the night. Some breeders send home a piece of bedding from where the pup slept with his littermates, and those familiar scents are a great comfort for the puppy on his first night without his siblings.

He will probably whine or cry. The puppy is objecting to the confinement and the fact that he is alone for the first time. This can be a stressful time for you as well as for the pup. It's important that you remain strong and don't let the puppy out of his crate to comfort him. He will fall asleep eventually. If you release him, the puppy will learn that crying means "out" and will continue that habit. You are laying the groundwork for future habits. Some breeders find that soft music can soothe a crying pup and help him get to sleep.

Valuable early socialization takes place among littermates, where rules of the pack are learned through wrestling and roughhousing, all in good fun.

SOCIALIZING YOUR PUPPY

The first 20 weeks of your Norwegian Elkhound puppy's life are the most important of his entire lifetime. A properly socialized puppy will grow up to be a confident and stable adult who will be a pleasure to live with and a welcome addition to the neighborhood.

The importance of socialization cannot be overemphasized. Research on canine behavior has proven that puppies who are not exposed to new sights, sounds, people and animals during their first 20 weeks of life will grow up to be timid and fearful, even aggressive, and unable to flourish outside of their familiar home environment.

Socializing your puppy is not difficult and, in fact, will be a fun time for you both. Lead training goes hand in hand with socialization, so your puppy will be learning how to walk on a lead at the same time that he's meeting the neighborhood. Because the Norwegian Elkhound is such a terrific breed, everyone will enjoy meeting "the new kid on the block." Take him for short walks, to the park and to other dog-friendly places where he will encounter new people, especially children. Puppies automatically recognize children as "little people" and are drawn to play with them. Just make sure that you supervise these meetings and that the children do not get too rough or encourage him to play too hard. An overzealous pup can often nip too hard, frightening the child and in turn making the puppy overly excited. A bad experience in puppyhood can impact a dog for life, so a pup that has a negative experience with a child may grow up to be shy or even aggressive around children.

Take your puppy along on your daily errands. Puppies are natural "people magnets," and most people who see your pup will want to pet him. All of these encounters will help to mold him into a confident adult dog. Likewise, you will soon feel like a confident, responsible dog owner, rightly proud of your mannerly Norwegian Elkhound.

Be especially careful of your puppy's encounters and experiences during the eight- to ten-week-old period, which is also called the "fear period." This is a serious imprinting period, and all contact during this time should be gentle and positive. A frightening or negative event could leave a

Just as in the wild, the adults keep watch over the pups as the youngsters get a taste of freedom (within safe confines, of course).

FIRST CAR RIDE

The ride to your home from the breeder will likely be your puppy's first automobile experience, and you should make every effort to keep him comfortable and secure. Bring a large towel or small blanket for the puppy to lie on during the trip and an extra towel in case the pup gets carsick or has a potty accident. It's best to have another person with you to hold the puppy in his lap. Most puppies will fall fast asleep from the rolling motion of the car. If the ride is lengthy, you may have to stop so that the puppy can relieve himself, so be sure to bring a leash, a collar and cleanup materials for those stops. Avoid rest areas for potty trips, since those are frequented by many dogs, who may carry parasites or disease. It's better to stop at grassy areas near gas stations or shopping centers to prevent unhealthy exposure for your pup.

permanent impression that could affect his future behavior if a similar situation arises.

Also make sure that your puppy has received his first and second rounds of vaccinations before you expose him to other dogs or bring him to places that other dogs may frequent. Avoid dog parks and other strange-dog areas until your vet assures you that your puppy is fully immunized and resistant to the diseases that can be passed between canines. Discuss safe early socialization with your vet and breeder, as some breeders recommend socializing the puppy even before he has received all of his inoculations.

TEETHING TIME

All puppies chew. It's normal canine behavior. Chewing just plain feels good to a puppy, especially during the three- to five-month teething period when the adult teeth are breaking through the gums. Rather than attempting to eliminate such a strong natural chewing instinct, you will be more successful if you redirect it and teach your puppy what he may or may not chew. Correct inappropriate chewing with a sharp "No!" and offer him a chew toy, praising him when he takes it. Don't become discouraged. Chewing usually decreases after the adult teeth have come in.

LEADER OF THE PUPPY'S PACK

Like other canines, your puppy needs an authority figure, someone he can look up to and regard as the leader of his "pack." His first pack leader was his dam, who taught him to be polite and not chew too hard on her ears or nip at her muzzle. He learned those same lessons from his littermates. If he played too rough, they cried in pain and stopped the game, which sent an important message to the rowdy puppy.

As puppies play together, they are also struggling to determine who will be the boss. Being pack animals, dogs need someone to be in charge. If a litter of puppies remained together beyond puppyhood, one of the pups would emerge as the strongest one, the one who calls the shots.

Once your puppy leaves the pack, he will look intuitively for a new leader. If he does not recognize you as that leader, he will try to assume that position for himself. Of course, it is hard to imagine your adorable Norwegian Elkhound puppy trying to be in charge when he is so small and seemingly helpless. You must remember that these are natural canine instincts. Do not cave in and allow your pup to get the upper "paw"!

Just as socialization is so important during these first 20 weeks, so too is your puppy's early education. He was born without any bad habits. He does not know what is good or bad behavior. If he does things like nipping and digging, it's because he is having fun and doesn't know that humans consider these things as "bad." It's your job to teach him proper puppy manners, and this is the best time to accomplish that—before he has developed bad habits, since it is much more difficult to "unlearn" or correct unacceptable learned behavior than to teach good behavior from the start.

Make sure that all members of the family understand the importance of being consistent when training their new puppy. If you tell the puppy to stay off the sofa and your daughter allows him to cuddle on the couch to watch her favorite television show, your pup will be confused about what he is and is not allowed to do. Have a family conference before your pup comes home so that everyone understands the basic principles of puppy training and the rules you have set forth for the pup, and agrees to follow them.

The old saying that "an ounce of prevention is worth a pound of cure" is especially true when it comes to puppies. It is much easier to prevent inappropriate behavior than it is to change it. It's also easier and less stressful for the pup, since it will keep discipline to a minimum and create a more positive learning environment for him. That, in turn, will also be easier on you!

Here are a few commonsense tips to keep your belongings safe and your puppy out of trouble:

- Keep your closet doors closed and your shoes, socks and other apparel off the floor so your puppy can't get at them.
- Keep a secure lid on the trash container or put the trash where your puppy can't dig into it. He can't damage what he can't reach!
- Supervise your puppy at all times to make sure he is not getting into mischief. If he starts to chew the corner of the rug, you can distract him instantly by tossing a toy for him to fetch. You also will be able to whisk him outside when you notice that he is about to piddle on the carpet. If you can't see your puppy, you can't teach him or correct his behavior.

While chewing is necessary for a teething pup, it's also a favorite leisure activity for the adult, as shown by this Norwegian Elkhound who is all settled in for a good chew.

PROPER CARE OF YOUR NORWEGIAN ELKHOUND

Adding a Norwegian Elkhound to your household means adding a new family member who will need your care each and every day. When your Norwegian Elkhound pup first comes home, you will start a routine with him so that, as he grows up, your dog will have a daily schedule just as you do. The aspects of your dog's daily care will likewise become regular parts of your day, so you'll both have a new schedule. Dogs learn by consistency and thrive on routine: regular times for meals, exercise, grooming and potty trips are just as important for your dog as they are for you! Your dog's schedule will depend much on your family's daily routine, but remember that you now have a new member of the family who is part of your day every day!

NOT HUNGRY?

No dog in his right mind would turn down his dinner, would he? If you notice that your dog has lost interest in his food, there could be any number of causes. Dental problems are a common cause of appetite loss, one that is often overlooked. If your dog has a toothache, a loose tooth or sore gums from infection, chances are it doesn't feel so good to chew. Think about when you've had a toothache! If your dog does not approach the food bowl with his usual enthusiasm, look inside his mouth for signs of a problem. Whatever the cause, you'll want to consult your vet so that your chow hound can get back to his happy, hungry self as soon as possible.

FEEDING

Feeding your dog the best diet is based on various factors, including age, activity level, overall condition and size of breed. When you first visit the breeder, he will share with you his advice about the proper diet for your dog based on his experience with the Elkhound and the foods with which he has had success. Likewise, your vet will be a helpful source of advice throughout the dog's life and will aid you in planning a diet for optimal health.

FEEDING THE PUPPY

Of course, your pup's very first food will be his dam's milk. There may be special situations in which pups fail to nurse, necessitating that the breeder hand-feed them with a formula, but for the most part pups spend the first weeks of life nursing from their dam. The breeder weans the pups by gradually introducing solid foods and decreasing the milk meals. Pups may even start themselves off on the weaning process, albeit inadvertently, if they snatch bites from their mom's food bowl.

By the time the pups are ready for new homes, they are fully weaned and eating a good puppy food. A good breeder will send you home with a diet sheet, detailing your pup's diet changes as he grows. As a new owner, you may be thinking, "Great! The breeder has taken care of the hard part." Not so fast.

A puppy's first year of life is the time when all or most of his growth and development takes place. This is a delicate time, and diet plays a huge role in proper skeletal and muscular formation. Improper diet and exercise habits can lead to damaging problems that will compromise the dog's health and movement for his entire life. That being said, new owners should not worry needlessly. With the myriad types of food formulated specifically for growing pups of different-sized breeds, dog-food manufacturers have taken much of the guesswork out of feeding your puppy well. Since growth-food formulas are designed to provide the nutrition that a growing puppy needs, it is unnecessary and, in fact, can prove harmful to add supplements to the diet. Research has shown that too much of certain vitamin supplements and minerals predispose a dog to skeletal problems. It's by no means a case of "if a little is good, a lot is better." At every stage of your dog's life, too much or too little in the way of nutrients can be harmful, which is why a manufactured complete food is the easiest way to know that your dog is getting what he needs.

The breeder sees the pups through weaning and starts them off on a good-quality puppy food.

Because of a young pup's small body and accordingly small digestive system, his daily portion will be divided up into small meals throughout the day. This can mean starting off with three or more meals a day and decreasing the number of meals as the pup matures. For the adult dog, dividing the day's food into two meals on a morning/evening schedule is healthier for the dog's digestion than feeding one large daily portion.

Regarding the feeding schedule, feeding the pup at the same times and in the same place each day is important for both housebreaking purposes and establishing the dog's everyday routine. As for the amount to feed, growing puppies generally need proportionately more food per body weight than their adult counterparts, but a pup should never be allowed to gain excess weight. Dogs of all ages should be kept in proper body condition, but extra weight can strain a pup's developing frame, causing skeletal problems.

Watch your pup's weight as he grows and, if the recommended amounts seem to be too much or too little for your pup, consult the vet about appropriate dietary changes. Keep in mind that treats, although small, can quickly add up throughout the day, contributing unnecessary calories. Treats are fine when used prudently; opt for dog treats specially formulated to be healthy or for nutritious snacks like small pieces of cheese or cooked chicken.

SWITCHING FOODS

There are certain times in a dog's life when it becomes necessary to switch his food; for example, from puppy to adult food and then from adult to senior-dog food. Additionally, you may decide to feed your pup a different type of food from what he received from the breeder, and there may be "emergency" situations in which you can't find your dog's normal brand and have to offer something else temporarily. Anytime a change is made, for whatever reason, the switch must be done gradually. You don't want to upset the dog's stomach or end up with a picky eater who refuses to eat something new. A tried-and-true approach is, over the course of about a week, to mix a little of the new food in with the old, increasing the proportion of new to old as the days progress. At the end of the week, you'll be feeding his regular portions of the new food, and he will barely notice the change.

Feeding the Adult Dog

For the adult (meaning physically mature) dog, feeding properly is about maintenance, not growth. An Elkhound can usually switch to an adult food around 12 months of age, depending on the individual dog, although he is still developing physically. Again, correct weight is a concern. Your dog should appear fit and should have an evident "waist." His ribs should not be protruding (a sign of being underweight), but they should be covered by only a slight layer of fat. Under normal circumstances, an adult dog can be maintained fairly easily with a high-quality nutritionally complete adult-formula food.

Factor treats into your dog's overall daily caloric intake, and avoid offering table scraps. Certain "people foods," including chocolate, nuts, onions, grapes and raisins, are actually toxic to dogs, not to mention that feeding table scraps encourages begging and overeating. Most Norwegian Elkhounds are good eaters and thoroughly enjoy their food; indeed, some would say they are greedy dogs. However, they do make good use of the food they eat and, pound for pound, they do not actually require as much food as other breeds. Regardless, overweight dogs are more prone to health problems. Research has even shown that obesity takes years off a dog's life. With that in mind, resist the urge to overfeed and over-treat. Don't make additions to your dog's complete diet, whether with tidbits or with extra vitamins and minerals, unless advised by the vet.

The amount of food needed for proper maintenance will vary depending on your individual dog's activity level, but you will be able to tell whether the daily portions are keeping him in good shape. With the wide variety of good complete foods available,

Elkhound siblings enjoy their dinner and each other's company.

DIET DON'TS

- Got milk? Don't give it to your dog! Dogs cannot tolerate large quantities of cows' milk, as they do not have the enzymes to digest lactose.
- You may have heard of dog owners who add raw eggs to their dogs' food for a shiny coat or to make the food more palatable, but consumption of raw eggs too often can cause a deficiency of the vitamin biotin.
- Avoid feeding table scraps, as they will upset the balance of the dog's complete food. Additionally, fatty or highly seasoned foods can cause upset canine stomachs.
- Do not offer raw meat to your dog. Raw meat can contain parasites; it also is high in fat.
- Vitamin A toxicity in dogs can be caused by too much raw liver, especially if the dog already gets enough vitamin A in his balanced diet, which should be the case.
- Bones like chicken, pork chop and other soft bones are not suitable, as they easily splinter.

choosing what to feed is largely a matter of personal preference. Just as with the puppy, the adult dog should have consistency in his mealtimes and feeding place. In addition to a consistent routine, regular mealtimes also allow you to see how much your Elkhound is eating. If the dog seems never to be satisfied or, likewise, becomes uninterested in his food, you will know right away that something is wrong and can consult the vet. Scheduled meals also allow you to give your Elkhound some quiet time before and after mealtimes, something that is healthy for all dogs.

Diets for the Aging Dog

A good rule of thumb is that once a dog has reached 75% of his expected lifespan, he has reached "senior citizen" or geriatric status. Your Norwegian Elkhound will be considered a senior at about 8 years of age; he has a projected lifespan of about 12 years, hopefully longer.

What does aging have to do with your dog's diet? No, he won't get a discount at the local diner's early-bird special. Yes, he will require some dietary changes to accommodate the changes that come along with increased age. One change is that the older dog's dietary needs become more similar to that of a puppy. Specifically, dogs can metabolize more protein as youngsters and seniors than in the adult-maintenance stage. Discuss with your vet whether you need to switch to a higher-protein or senior-formulated food or whether your current adult-dog food contains sufficient nutrition for the senior.

Watching the dog's weight remains essential, even more so in the senior stage. Older dogs are already more vulnerable to illness, and obesity only contributes to their susceptibility to problems. As the older dog becomes less active and, thus, exercises less, his regular portions may cause him to gain weight. At this point, you may consider decreasing his daily food intake or switching to a reduced-calorie food. As with other changes, you should consult your vet for advice.

Don't allow your Elkhound to help himself to a snack! If you don't want him to eat it, keep it out of reach.

Types of Food and Reading Labels

When selecting the type of food to feed your dog, it is important to check out labels to determine the ingredients in the different foods. Many dry-food products have soybean, corn or rice as the main ingredient. The main ingredient will be listed first on the label, with the rest of the ingredients following in descending order according to their proportion in the food. While these types of dry food are fine, dry foods based on meat or fish are more commonly recommended. These are better-quality foods and thus higher priced. However, they may be just as economical in the long run because studies have shown that it takes less of a higher-quality food to maintain a dog.

Comparing the various types of food—dry, canned and semi-moist—dry foods contain the least amount of water and canned foods the most. Proportionately, dry foods are the most calorie- and nutrient-dense, which means that you need more of a canned-food product to supply the same amount of nutrition. In households with breeds of different size, the canned/dry/semi-moist question can be of special importance. Larger breeds obviously eat more than smaller ones and thus in general do better on dry foods, but smaller breeds do fine on canned foods and require "small

WEIGHT AND SEE!

When you look at yourself in the mirror each day, you get very used to what you see! It's only when you pull out last year's holiday outfit and can't zip it up that you notice that you've put on some pounds. Dog owners are the same way with their dogs. Often a few pounds go unnoticed, and it's not until some time passes or the vet remarks that your dog looks more than pleasantly plump that you realize what's happened. To avoid your pet's becoming obese right under your very nose, make a habit of routinely evaluating his condition with a hands-on test.

Can you feel, but not see, your dog's rib cage? Does your dog have a waist? His waist should be evident by touch and also visible from above and from the side. In top view, the dog's body should have an hourglass shape. These are indicators of good condition.

While it's not hard to spot an extremely skinny or overly rotund dog, it's the subtle changes that lead up to under- or overweight condition of which we must be aware. If your dog's ribs are visible, he is too thin. Conversely, if you can't feel the ribs under too much fat, and if there's no indication of a waistline, your dog is overweight. Both of these conditions require changes to the diet.
A trip or sometimes just a call to the vet will help you modify your dog's feeding.

bite" formulations to protect their small mouths and teeth if fed dry foods. So if you have different-sized breeds in your household, consider both your own preferences and what your dogs like to eat, but in general think canned for the little guys and dry or semi-moist for everyone else. You may find success mixing the food types as well. Water is important for all dogs, but even more so for those fed dry foods, as there is no high water content in their food.

There are strict controls that regulate the nutritional content of dog food, and a food has to meet the minimum requirements in order to be considered "complete and balanced." It is important that you choose such a food for your dog, so check the label to be sure that your chosen food meets the requirements. If not, look for a food that clearly states on the label that it is formulated to be complete and balanced for your dog's particular stage of life.

Maintaining an adult Elkhound in proper condition is fairly easy with a complete food in the right amounts and sufficient activity.

FEEDING IN HOT WEATHER

Even the most dedicated chow hound may have less of an appetite when the weather is hot or humid. If your dog leaves more of his food behind than usual, adjust his portions until the weather and his appetite return to normal. Never leave the uneaten portion in the bowl, hoping he will return to finish it, because higher temperatures encourage food spoilage and bacterial growth.

Recommendations for amounts to feed will also be indicated on the label. You should also ask your vet about proper food portions, and you will keep an eye on your dog's condition to see whether the recommended amounts are adequate. If he becomes over- or underweight, you will need to make adjustments; this also would be a good time to consult your vet.

The food label may also make feeding suggestions, such as whether moistening a dry-food product is recommended. Sometimes a splash of water will make the food more palatable for the dog and even enhance the flavor; it may also help a "chow hound" eat more slowly, which is better for his digestion. Don't be overwhelmed by the many factors that go into feeding your dog.

Manufacturers of complete and balanced foods make it easy, and once you find the right food and amounts for your Norwegian Elkhound, his daily feeding will be a matter of routine.

DON'T FORGET THE WATER!

Regardless of what type of food your Elkhound eats, there's no doubt that he needs plenty of water. Fresh cold water, in a clean bowl, should be freely available to your dog. There are special circumstances, such as during puppy housebreaking, when you will want to monitor your pup's water intake so that you will be able to predict when he will need to relieve himself, but water must be available to him nonetheless. Water is essential for hydration and proper body function just as it is in humans.

You will get to know how much your dog typically drinks in a day. Of course, in the heat or if exercising vigorously, he will be more thirsty and will drink more. However, if he begins to drink noticeably more water for no apparent reason, this could signal any of various problems, and you are advised to consult your vet.

Have a bowl of fresh water available to your Elkhound both indoors and outdoors.

Water is the best drink for dogs. Some owners are tempted to give milk from time to time or to moisten dry food with milk, but dogs do not have the enzymes necessary to digest the lactose in milk, which is much different from the milk that nursing puppies receive. Therefore stick with clean fresh water to quench your dog's thirst, and always have it readily available to him.

A COAT IN THE SUMMER

A dog's long or heavy coat is designed for insulation in any type of weather, so think again before giving your dog a summer haircut. Shaving down his coat in warm weather will affect his body's natural temperature regulation and is neither necessary nor beneficial.

EXERCISE

The Norwegian Elkhound is an active breed, so exercise is necessary for both its health and happiness, as well as for maintaining ideal muscular condition. How a Norwegian Elkhound is best exercised depends very much on the area in which you live. If possible, a good walk twice daily, with an opportunity for free run in a safe environment, should become routine in adulthood. Please remember, though, that puppies should have only limited, gentle exercise, particularly before the age of six months.

When allowing a dog to run free, safety is of utmost importance. For this reason, all possible escape routes should be thoroughly checked out and secured before letting your Norwegian Elkhound off the lead. Of course, your yard also needs to be safely enclosed by fencing, which should be checked at regular intervals.

The active and outdoor-loving Elkhound will enjoy plenty of exercise, especially if you get moving along with him.

Just as with anything else you do with your dog, you must set a routine for his exercise. It's the same as your daily morning run before work or never missing the 7 p.m. aerobics class. If you plan it and get into the habit of actually doing it, it will become just another part of your day. Think of it as making daily exercise appointments with your dog, and stick to your schedule. Remember that after vigorous exercise, a rest period should elapse before your dog is fed.

As a rule, Elkhounds in normal health should have at least two half-hour sessions of activity each day. Dogs with health or orthopedic problems may have specific limitations, so their exercise plans are best devised with the help of a vet. For healthy dogs, there are many ways to fit this activity into your day. Depending on your schedule, you may plan a walk or activity session in the morning and again in the evening, or you may plan one long session supplemented by shorter walks throughout the day. Walking is the most popular way to exercise a dog (it's good for you, too!); other suggestions include retrieving games, jogging and disc-catching or other active games with his toys. If you have a safe body of water nearby and a dog that likes to swim, swimming is an excellent form of exercise for dogs, putting no stress on his frame. An Elkhound will certainly accept more than an hour of daily exercise; he will enjoy the activity and be a more content dog, less apt to become bored and lapse into destructive behavior.

THAT'S ENTERTAINMENT!

Is your dog home alone for much of the day? If you haven't taught him how to crochet or play the French horn, then he'll probably need something to occupy his paws and jaws, lest he turn to chewing up the carpet and draperies. Recommended conditioning devices are toys that stimulate your dog both physically and mentally. Some of the most popular toys are those that are constructed to hide food inside. They provide not only a challenge but also instant gratification when your dog gets to the treat. Be sure to clean these carefully to prevent bacteria from building up.

Good daily exercise for an Elkhound means a couple of on-lead walks plus some time for free exercise in a secure area.

Bear in mind that an overweight dog should never be suddenly over-exercised; instead he should be encouraged to increase exercise slowly. And as we've mentioned, not only is exercise essential to keep the dog's body fit, it is essential to his mental well-being. A bored dog will find something to do, which often manifests itself in some type of destructive behavior. In this sense, exercise is just as essential for the owner's mental well-being!

GROOMING

Brushing

General grooming of a Norwegian Elkhound's coat is a simple procedure. However, because this breed sheds, grooming is very important; it should become a regular routine to aid in conditioning the coat. Initially using a

The Elkhound has a heavy, protective double coat that sheds, thus requiring brushing on a regular basis.

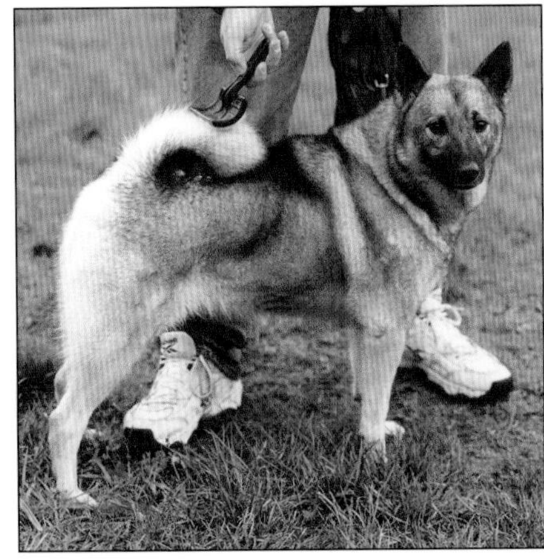
The tail is brushed in the direction in which it curls, over the dog's back.

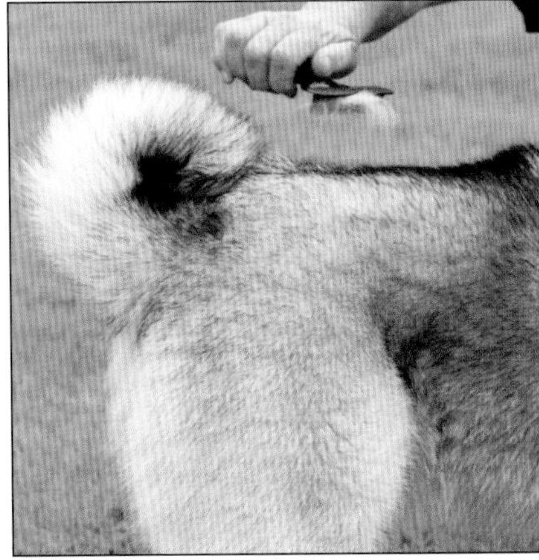
Loose and dead hairs are easily removed without any discomfort to the dog.

MUDDY BUDDY
Following a bath, some Elkhounds have an urge to roll around in the first available dirt or mud patch they find, completely undoing all the good work you have just done! It is wise to keep your dog away from dirt and soil until his coat is dry; otherwise, he will just need another bath!

slicker brush, brushing is done following the lay of the hair. It is a good idea to begin at the back of the neck, working backwards toward the tail and the trousers, always paying careful attention to not accidentally brush through a delicate part of the anatomy!

Following a thorough brushing with a slicker brush, a steel rake will help to remove any loose hairs and will separate the undercoat. A natural bristle brush is often used to give the final touch. This is also a useful brush to use on the head and legs, where the coat is shorter. Always keep in mind that the Norwegian Elkhound is essentially a natural breed and, although the dog should look smart, he should be presented in a natural way.

BATHING

How frequently you bathe your Norwegian Elkhound will depend very much on your own individual dog, and whether or not you show your dog. A Norwegian Elkhound needs to be exercised in all types of weather, so in wet weather and on muddy soil your dog will likely come back from a walk looking filthy. Although your Norwegian Elkhound's coat will repel mud, from time to time you will inevitably need to bathe your dog, or at least freshen up the legs and under the belly. If you show your Norwegian Elkhound, remember not to bathe him the day before a show; if you do, the coat will not have sufficient time to resume its normal texture.

If you give your dog his first bath when he is young, he will become accustomed to the process. Wrestling a dog into the tub or chasing a freshly shampooed dog who has escaped from the bath will be no fun! Most dogs don't naturally enjoy their baths, but you at least want yours to cooperate with you.

Before bathing the dog, have the items you'll need close at hand. First, decide where you will bathe the dog. You should have a tub or basin with a non-slip surface. In warm weather, some like to use a portable pool in the yard, but make sure that your dog doesn't head for the nearest dirt pile following his bath! You will also need a hose or shower spray to wet the coat thoroughly, a shampoo formulated for dogs and a few absorbent towels. Human shampoos are too harsh for dogs' coats and will dry them out.

Before wetting the dog, give him a brush-through to remove any dead hair, dirt and mats. Make sure he is at ease in the tub and have the water at a comfortable temperature. Begin bathing by wetting the coat all the way down to the skin. Massage in the shampoo, keeping it away from his face and eyes. Rinse him thoroughly, again avoiding the

WATER SHORTAGE

No matter how well behaved your dog is, bathing is always a project! Nothing can substitute for a good warm bath, but owners do have the option of giving their dogs "dry" baths. Pet shops sell excellent products, in both powder and spray forms, designed for spot-cleaning your dog. These dry shampoos are convenient for touch-up jobs when you don't have the time to bathe your dog in the traditional way.

Muddy feet, messy behinds and smelly coats can be spot-cleaned and deodorized with a "wet-nap"-style cleaner. On those days when your dog insists on rolling in fresh goose droppings and there's no time for a bath, a spot bath can save the day. These pre-moistened wipes are also handy for other grooming needs like wiping faces, ears and eyes and freshening tails and behinds.

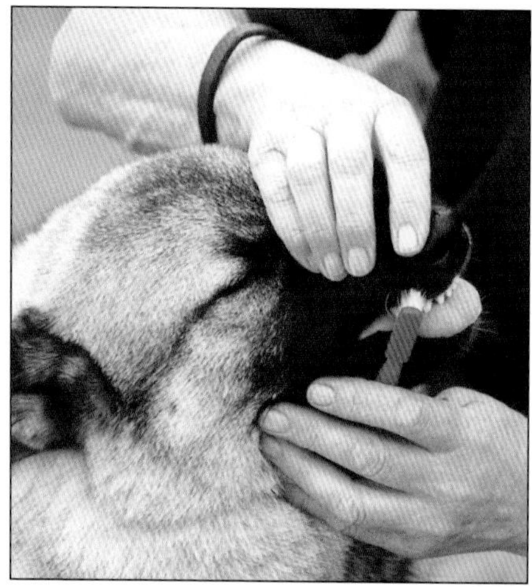

Along with regular exams by the vet, tooth cleaning at home is required to prevent dental problems.

eyes and ears, as you don't want to get water into the ear canals. A thorough rinsing is important, as shampoo residue is drying and itchy to the dog.

Drying your Elkhound with a hair dryer following a bath is not a good idea, as this will cause the coat to fluff up. More suitable for this breed is towel-drying. You can also use a chamois cloth to remove as much moisture as possible. Provided the day is warm and sunny, a good place to allow the dog to finish drying off is outside; otherwise keep him indoors and away from drafts until he is completely dry.

Nail Clipping

Having his nails trimmed is not on many dogs' lists of favorite things to do. With this in mind, you will need to accustom your puppy to the procedure at a young age so that he will sit still (well, as still as he can) for his pedicures. Long nails can cause the dog's feet to spread, which is not good for him; likewise, long nails can hurt if they unintentionally scratch, not good for you!

Some dogs' nails are worn down naturally by regular walking on hard surfaces, so the frequency with which you clip depends on your individual dog. Look at his nails from time to time and clip as needed; a good way to know when it's time for a trim is if you hear your dog clicking as he walks across the floor.

There are several types of nail clippers and even electric nail-grinding tools made for dogs; first we'll discuss using the clipper. To start, have your clipper ready and some doggie treats on hand. You want your pup to view his nail-clipping sessions in a positive light, and what better way to convince him than with food? You may want to enlist the help of an assistant to comfort the pup and offer treats as you concentrate on the clipping itself. The guillotine-type clipper is thought of by many as the easiest type to use; the nail tip is inserted into the opening, and blades on the top and bottom snip it off in one clip.

Start by grasping the pup's paw; a little pressure on the foot

SCOOTING HIS BOTTOM

Here's a doggy problem that many owners tend to neglect. If your dog is scooting his rear end around the carpet, he probably is experiencing anal-sac impaction or blockage. The anal sacs are the two grape-sized glands on either side of the dog's vent. The dog cannot empty these glands, which become filled with a foul-smelling material. The dog may attempt to lick the area to relieve the pressure. He may also rub his anus on your walls, furniture or floors.

Don't neglect your dog's rear end during grooming sessions. By squeezing both sides of the anus with a soft cloth, you can express some of the material in the sacs. If the material is pasty and thick, you likely will need the assistance of a veterinarian. Vets know how to express the glands and can show you how to do it correctly without hurting the dog or spraying yourself with the unpleasant liquid.

pad causes the nail to extend, making it easier to clip. Clip off a little at a time. If you can see the "quick," which is a blood vessel that runs through each nail, you will know how much to trim, as you do not want to cut into the quick. On that note, if you do cut the quick, which will cause bleeding, you can stem the flow of blood with a styptic pencil or other clotting agent. If you mistakenly nip the quick, do not panic or fuss, as this will cause the pup to be afraid. Simply reassure the pup, stop the bleeding and move on to the next nail. Don't be discouraged; you will become a professional canine pedicurist with practice.

You may or may not be able to see the quick, so it's best to just clip off a small bit at a time. If you see a dark dot in the center of the nail, this is the quick and your cue to stop clipping. Tell the puppy he's a "good boy" and offer a piece of treat with each nail. You can also use nail-clipping time to examine the footpads, making sure that they are not dry and cracked and that nothing has become embedded in them.

The nail grinder, the other choice, is many owners' first choice. Accustoming the puppy to the sound of the grinder and sensation of the buzz presents fewer challenges than the clipper, and there's no chance of cutting through the quick. Use the grinder on a low setting and always talk soothingly to your dog. He won't mind his salon visit, and he'll have nicely polished nails as well.

Ear Cleaning

While keeping your dog's ears clean unfortunately will not cause him to "hear" your commands any better, it will

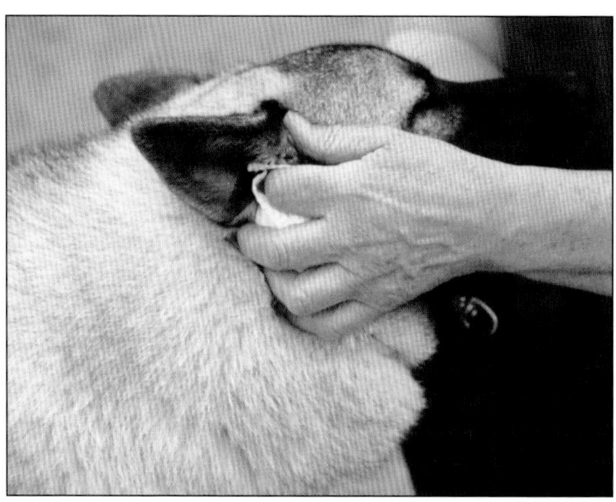

Clean your Elkhound's ears with a cotton wipe and suitable ear powder or liquid cleaning formula.

protect him from ear infection and ear-mite infestation. In addition, a dog's ears are vulnerable to waxy build-up and to collecting foreign matter from the outdoors. Look in your Elkhound's ears regularly to ensure that they look pink, clean and otherwise healthy. Even if they look fine, an odor in the ears signals a problem and means it's time to call the vet.

Fortunately, most Elkhound owners cite little or no trouble with their dogs' ears. Clean the ears as needed; using a cotton ball or pad, and never probing into the ear canal, wipe the ear gently. You can use an ear-cleansing liquid or powder available from your vet or pet-supply store; alternatively, you might prefer to use home-made solutions with ingredients like one part white vinegar and one part hydrogen peroxide. However, ask your vet about home remedies before you attempt to concoct something on your own!

Keep your dog's ears free of excess hair by plucking it as needed. If done gently, this will be painless for the dog. Look for wax, brown droppings (a sign of ear mites), redness or any other abnormalities. At the first sign of a problem, contact your vet so that he can prescribe an appropriate medication.

Eye Care

During grooming sessions, pay attention to the condition of your dog's eyes. Most Elkhounds stay clean around the eyes, but if soiling or tear staining has occurred, there are various cleaning agents made especially for this purpose. Look at the dog's eyes to make sure no debris has entered, especially after time spent outdoors.

The signs of an eye infection are obvious: mucus, redness, puffiness, scabs or other signs of irritation. If your dog's eyes become infected, the vet will likely prescribe an antibiotic ointment for treatment. If you notice signs of more serious problems, such as opacities in the eye, which usually indicate cataracts, consult the vet at once. Taking time to pay attention to your dog's eyes will alert you in the early stages of any problem so that you can get your dog treatment as soon as possible. You could save your dog's sight!

IDENTIFICATION AND TRAVEL

ID for Your Dog

You love your Norwegian Elkhound and want to keep him safe. Of course you take every precaution to prevent his escaping from the yard or becoming lost or stolen. You have a sturdy high fence and you always keep your dog on lead when out and about in public places. If your dog is not properly identified, however, you are overlooking a major aspect of his safety. We hope to never be in a situation where our dog is missing, but we should practice prevention in the unfortunate case that this happens; identification greatly increases the chances of your dog's being returned to you.

There are several ways to identify your dog. First, the traditional dog tag should be a staple in your dog's wardrobe, attached to his everyday collar. Tags can be made of sturdy plastic and various metals and should include your contact information so that a person who finds the dog can get in touch with you right away to arrange his return. Many people today enjoy the wide range of decorative tags available, so have fun and create a tag to match your dog's personality. Of course, it is important that the tag stays on the collar, so have a secure "O" ring attachment; you also can explore the type of tag that slides right onto the collar.

In you go! This Norwegian Elkhound is secure in his crate for a safe car ride.

In addition to the ID tag, which every dog should wear even if identified by another method, two other forms of identification have become popular:

microchipping and tattooing. In microchipping, a tiny scannable chip is painlessly inserted under the dog's skin. The number is registered to you so that, if your lost dog turns up at a clinic or shelter, the chip can be scanned to retrieve your contact information.

The advantage of the microchip is that it is a permanent form of ID, but there are some factors to consider. Several different companies make microchips, and not all are compatible with the others' scanning devices. It's best to find a company with a universal microchip that can be read by scanners made by other companies as well. It won't do any good to have the dog chipped if the information cannot be retrieved. Also, not every humane society, shelter and clinic is equipped with a scanner, although more and more facilities are equipping themselves. In fact, many shelters microchip dogs that they adopt out to new homes.

Because the microchip is not visible to the eye, the dog must wear a tag that states that he is microchipped so that whoever picks him up will know to have him scanned. He of course also should have a tag with contact information in case his chip cannot be read. Humane societies and veterinary clinics offer microchipping service, which is usually very affordable.

Though less popular than microchipping, tattooing is another permanent method of ID for dogs. Most vets perform this service, and there are also clinics that perform dog tattooing. This is also an affordable procedure and one that will not cause much discomfort for the dog. It is best to put the tattoo in a visible area, such as the ear, to deter theft. It is sad to say that there are cases of dogs' being stolen and sold to research laboratories, but such laboratories will not accept tattooed dogs.

To ensure that the tattoo is effective in aiding your dog's return to you, the tattoo number must be registered with a national organization. That way, when someone finds a tattooed dog, a phone call to the registry will quickly match the dog with his owner.

PET OR STRAY?

Besides the obvious benefit of providing your contact information to whoever finds your lost dog, an ID tag makes your dog more approachable and more likely to be recovered. A strange dog wandering the neighborhood without a collar and tags will look like a stray, while the collar and tags indicate that the dog is someone's pet. Even if the ID tags become detached from the collar, the collar alone will make a person more likely to pick up the dog.

Hit the Road

Car travel with your Norwegian Elkhound may be limited to necessity only, such as trips to the vet, or you may bring your dog along almost everywhere you go. This will depend much on your individual dog and how he reacts to rides in the car. You can begin desensitizing your dog to car travel as a pup so that it's something that he's used to. Still, some dogs suffer from motion sickness. Your vet may prescribe a medication for this if trips in the car pose a problem for your dog. At the very least, you will need to get him to the vet, so he will need to tolerate these trips with the least amount of hassle possible.

DOGGONE!
Wendy Ballard is the editor and publisher of the *DogGone*™ newsletter, which comes out bi-monthly and features fun articles by dog owners who love to travel with their dogs. The newsletter includes information about fun places to go with your dogs, including popular vacation spots, dog-friendly hotels, parks, campgrounds, resorts, etc., as well as interesting activities to do with your dog, such as flyball, agility and much more. You can subscribe to the publication by contacting the publisher at PO Box 651155, Vero Beach, FL 32965-1155.

Start taking your pup on short trips, maybe just around the block to start. If he is fine with short trips, lengthen your rides a little at a time. Start to take him on your errands or just for drives around town. By this time it will be easy to tell whether your dog is a born traveler or would prefer staying at home when you are on the road.

Of course, safety is a concern for dogs in the car. First, he must travel securely, not left loose to roam about the car where he could be injured or distract the driver. A young pup can be held by a passenger initially but should soon graduate to a travel crate, which can be the same crate he uses in the home. Other options include a car harness (like a seat belt for dogs) and partitioning the back of the car with a gate made for this purpose.

Bring along what you will need for the dog. He should wear his collar and ID tags, of course, and you should bring his leash, water (and food if a long trip) and clean-up materials for potty breaks and in case of motion sickness. Always keep your dog on his leash when you make stops, and never leave him alone in the car. Many a dog has died from the heat inside a closed car; this does not take much time at all. A dog left alone inside a car can also be a target for thieves.

TRAINING YOUR
NORWEGIAN ELKHOUND

BASIC TRAINING PRINCIPLES: PUPPY VS. ADULT

There's a big difference between training an adult dog and training a young puppy. With a young puppy, everything is new! At eight to ten weeks of age, he will be experiencing many things, and he has nothing with which to compare these experiences. Up to this point, he has been with his dam and littermates, not one-on-one with people except in his interactions with his breeder and visitors to the litter.

When you first bring the puppy home, he is eager to please you. This means that he accepts doing things your way. During the next couple of months, he will absorb the basis of everything he needs to know for the rest of his life. This early age is even referred to as the "sponge" stage. After that, for the next 18 months, it's up to you to reinforce good manners by building on the foundation that you've established. Once your puppy is reliable in basic commands and behavior and has reached the appropriate age, you may gradually introduce him to some of the interesting sports, games and activities available to pet owners and their dogs.

Raising your puppy is a family affair. Each member of the family must know what rules to set forth for the puppy and how to use the same one-word commands to mean exactly the same thing every time. Even if yours is a large family, one person will soon be considered by the pup to be the leader, the alpha person in his pack, the "boss" who must be obeyed. Often that highly regarded person turns out to be the one who feeds the puppy.

CREATURES OF HABIT

Canine behaviorists and trainers aptly describe dogs as "creatures of habit," meaning that dogs respond to structure in their daily lives and welcome a routine. Do not interpret this to mean that dogs enjoy endless repetition in their training sessions. Dogs get bored just as humans do. Keep training sessions interesting and exciting. Vary the commands and the locations in which you practice. Give short breaks for play in between lessons. A bored student will never be the best performer in the class.

Food ranks very high on the puppy's list of important things! That's why your puppy is rewarded with small treats along with verbal praise when he responds to you correctly. As the puppy learns to do what you want him to do, the food rewards are gradually eliminated and only the praise remains. If you were to keep up with the food treats, you could have two problems on your hands—an obese dog and a beggar.

Training begins the minute your Norwegian Elkhound puppy steps through the doorway of your home, so don't make the mistake of putting the puppy on the floor and telling him by your actions to "Go for it! Run wild!" Even if this is your first puppy, you must act as if you know what you're doing: be the boss. An uncertain pup may be terrified to move, while a bold one will be ready to take you at your word and start plotting to destroy the house! Before you collected your puppy, you decided where his own special place would be, and that's where to put him when you first arrive home. Give him a house tour after he has investigated his area and had a nap and a bathroom "pit stop."

SHOULD WE ENROLL?

If you have the means and the time, you should definitely take your dog to obedience classes. Begin with puppy kindergarten classes in which puppies of all sizes learn basic lessons while getting the opportunity to meet and greet each other; it's as much about socialization as it is about good manners. What you learn in class you can practice at home. And if you goof up in practice, you'll get help in the next session.

It's worth mentioning here that, if you've adopted an adult dog that is completely trained to your liking, lucky you! You're off the hook! However, if that dog spent his life up to this point in a kennel, or even in a good home but without any real training, be prepared to tackle the job ahead. A dog three years of age or older with no previous training cannot be blamed for not knowing what he was never taught. While the dog is trying to understand and

BASIC PRINCIPLES OF DOG TRAINING

1. Start training early. A young puppy is ready, willing and able.
2. Timing is your all-important tool. Praise at the exact time that the dog responds correctly. Pay close attention.
3. Patience is almost as important as timing!
4. Repeat! The same word has to mean the same thing every time.
5. In the beginning, praise all correct behavior verbally, along with treats and petting.

learn your rules, at the same time he has to unlearn many of his previously self-taught habits and general view of the world.

Working with a professional trainer will speed up your progress with an adopted adult dog. You'll need patience, too. Some new rules may be close to impossible for the dog to accept. After all, he's been successful so far by doing everything his way! (Patience again.) He may agree with your instruction for a few days and then slip back into his old ways, so you must be just as consistent and understanding in your teaching as you would be with a puppy. (More patience needed yet again!) Your dog has to learn to pay attention to your voice, your family, the daily routine, new smells, new sounds and, in some cases, even a new climate.

One of the most important things to find out about a newly adopted adult dog is his reaction to children (yours and others), strangers and your friends, and how he acts upon meeting other dogs. If he was not socialized with dogs as a puppy, this could be a major problem. This does not mean that he's a "bad" dog, a vicious dog or an aggressive dog; rather, it means that he has no idea how to read another dog's body language. There's no way for him to tell whether the other dog is a friend or foe. Survival instinct takes over, telling him to attack first and ask questions later. This definitely calls for professional help and, even then, may not be a behavior that can be corrected 100% reliably (or even at all). If you have a puppy, this is why it is so very important to introduce your young puppy properly to other puppies and "dog-friendly" adult dogs.

HOUSE-TRAINING YOUR NORWEGIAN ELKHOUND

Dogs are tactility-oriented when it comes to house-training. In other words, they respond to the surface on which they are given approval to eliminate. The choice is yours (the dog's version is in parentheses): The lawn (including the neighbors' lawns)? A bare patch of earth under a tree (where people like to sit and relax in the summertime)? Concrete steps or patio (all sidewalks, garages and basement floors)? The curbside (watch out for cars)? A small area of crushed stone in a corner of the yard (mine!)? The latter is the best choice if you can manage it, because it will remain strictly for the dog's use and is easy to keep clean.

You can start out with paper-training indoors and switch over to an outdoor surface as the puppy matures and gains control over his need to eliminate. For the nay-sayers, don't worry—this won't mean that the dog will soil on every piece of newspaper lying around the house. You are training him to go outside, remember? Starting out by paper-training often is the only choice for a city dog.

During housebreaking, keeping an eye on your pup's water intake will help you predict his potty needs, as what goes in comes out rather quickly.

> **TIME TO PLAY!**
>
> Playtime can happen both indoors and out. A young puppy is growing so rapidly that he needs sleep more than he needs a lot of physical exercise. Puppies get sufficient exercise on their own just through normal puppy activity. Monitor play with young children so you can remove the puppy when he's had enough, or calm the kids if they get too rowdy. Almost all puppies love to chase after a toy you've thrown, and you can turn your games into educational activities. Every time your puppy brings the toy back to you, say "Give it" (or "Drop it") followed by "Good dog" and throwing it again. If he's reluctant to give it to you, offer a small treat so that he drops the toy as he takes the treat. He will soon get the idea.

When Your Puppy's "Got to Go"

Your puppy's need to relieve himself is seemingly non-stop, but signs of improvement will be seen each week. From 8 to 10 weeks old, the puppy will have to be taken outside every time he wakes up, about 10–15 minutes after every meal and after every period of play—all day long, from first thing in the morning until his bedtime! That's a total of ten or more trips per day to teach the puppy where it's okay to relieve

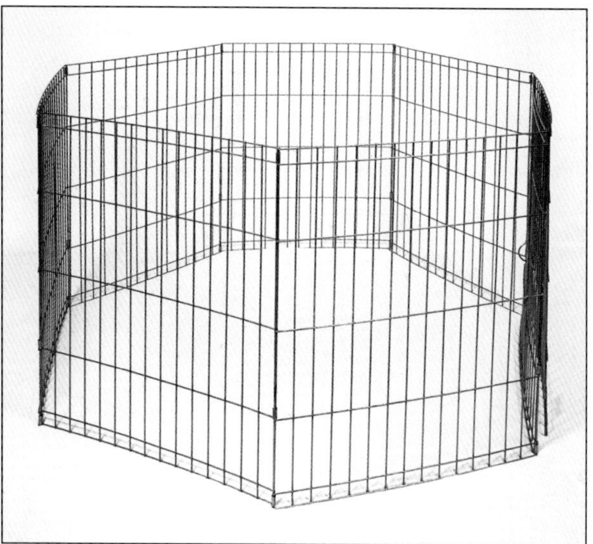

A wire pen, high enough so pup can't climb out and sturdy enough that pup can't knock it down, is a helpful aid in safely confining your puppy.

himself. With that schedule in mind, you can see that house-training a young puppy is not a part-time job. It requires someone to be home all day.

If that seems overwhelming or impossible, do a little planning. For example, plan to pick up your puppy at the start of a vacation period. If you can't get home in the middle of the day, plan to hire a dog-sitter or ask a neighbor to come over to take the pup outside, feed him his lunch and then take him out again about ten or so minutes after he's eaten. Also make arrangements with that or another person to be your "emergency" contact if you have to stay late on the job. Remind yourself—repeatedly—that this hectic schedule improves as the puppy gets older.

Home within a Home

Your Norwegian Elkhound puppy needs to be confined to one secure, puppy-proof area when no one is able to watch his every move. Generally, the kitchen is the place of choice because the floor is washable. Likewise, it's a busy family area that will accustom the pup to a variety of noises, everything from pots and pans to the telephone, blender and dishwasher. He will also be enchanted by the smell of your cooking (and will never be critical when you burn something). An exercise pen (also called an "ex-pen," a puppy version of a playpen) within the room of choice is an excellent means of

DAILY SCHEDULE

How many relief trips does your puppy need per day? A puppy up to the age of 14 weeks will need to go outside about 8 to 12 times per day! You will have to take the pup out any time he starts sniffing around the floor or turning in small circles, as well as after naps, meals, games and lessons or whenever he's released from his crate. Once the puppy is 14 to 22 weeks of age, he will require only 6 to 8 relief trips. At the ages of 22 to 32 weeks, the puppy will require about 5 to 7 trips. Adult dogs typically require 4 relief trips per day, in the morning, afternoon, evening and late at night.

EXTRA! EXTRA!

The headlines read: "Puppy Piddles Here!" Breeders commonly use newspapers to line their whelping pens, so puppies learn to associate newspapers with relieving themselves. Do not use newspapers to line your pup's crate, as this will signal to your puppy that it is OK to urinate in his crate. If you choose to paper-train your puppy, you will layer newspapers on a section of the floor near the door he uses to go outside. You should encourage the puppy to use the papers to relieve himself, and bring him there whenever you see him getting ready to go. Little by little, you will reduce the size of the newspaper-covered area so that the puppy will learn to relieve himself "on the other side of the door."

confinement for a young pup. He can see out and has a certain amount of space in which to run about, but he is safe from dangerous things like electrical cords, heating units, trash baskets or open kitchen-supply cabinets. Place the pen where the puppy will not get a blast of heat or air conditioning.

In the pen, you can put a few toys, his bed (which can be his crate if the dimensions of pen and crate are compatible) and a few layers of newspaper in one small corner, just in case. A water bowl can be hung at a convenient height on the side of the ex-pen so it won't become a splashing pool for an innovative puppy. His food dish can go on the floor, next to the water bowl.

Crates are something that pet owners are at last getting used to for their dogs. Wild or domestic canines have always preferred to sleep in den-like safe spots, and that is exactly what the crate provides. How often have you seen adult dogs that choose to sleep under a table or chair even though they have full run of the house? It's the den connection.

In your "happy" voice, use the word "Crate" every time you put the pup into his den. If he's new to a crate, toss in a small biscuit for him to chase the first few times. At night, after he's been outside, he should sleep in his crate. The crate may be kept in his designated area at night or, if you want to be sure to hear those

A dog will follow his nose to locate his relief spot over and over again.

wake-up yips in the morning, put the crate in a corner of your bedroom. However, don't make any response whatsoever to whining or crying. If he's completely ignored, he'll settle down and get to sleep.

Good bedding for a young puppy is an old folded bath towel or an old blanket, something that is easily washable and disposable if necessary ("accidents" will happen!). Never put newspaper in the puppy's crate. Also, those old ideas about adding a clock to replace his mother's heartbeat, or a hot-water bottle to replace her warmth, are just that—old ideas. The clock could drive the puppy nuts, and the hot-water bottle could end up as a very soggy waterbed! An extremely good

A fenced yard is so helpful in house-training. Once puppy has learned where in the yard his potty spot is, he can be let out on his own to do his business.

breeder would have introduced your puppy to the crate by letting two pups sleep together for a couple of nights, followed by several nights alone. How thankful you will be if you found that breeder!

Safe toys in the pup's crate or area will keep him occupied, but monitor their condition closely. Discard any toys that show signs of being chewed to bits. Squeaky parts, bits of stuffing or plastic or any other small pieces can cause intestinal blockage or possibly choking if swallowed.

It's best to train your Elkhound to an out-of-the way spot, away from walkways and places in the yard that people frequent.

LEASH TRAINING

House-training and leash training go hand in hand, literally. When taking your puppy outside to do his business, lead him there on his leash. Unless an emergency potty run is called for, do not whisk the puppy up into your arms and take him outside. If you have a fenced yard, you have the advantage of letting the puppy loose to go out, but it's better to put the dog on the leash and take him to his designated place in the yard until he is reliably house-trained. Taking the puppy for a walk is the best way to house-train a dog. The dog will associate the walk with his time to relieve himself, and the exercise of walking stimulates the dog's bowels and bladder. Dogs that are not trained to relieve themselves on a walk may hold it until they get back home, which of course defeats half the purpose of the walk.

PROGRESSING WITH POTTY-TRAINING

After you've taken your puppy out and he has relieved himself in the area you've selected, he can have some free time with the family as long as there is someone responsible for watching him. That doesn't mean just someone in the same room who is watching TV or busy on the computer, but one person who is doing nothing other than keeping an eye on the pup, playing with him on the floor and helping him understand his position in the pack.

This first taste of freedom will let you begin to set the house rules. If you don't want the dog on the furniture, now is the time to prevent his first attempts to jump up onto the couch. The word to use in this case is "Off," not "Down." "Down" is the word you will use to teach the down position, which is something entirely different.

Most corrections at this stage come in the form of simply distracting the puppy. Instead of telling him "No" for "Don't chew the carpet," distract the chomping puppy with a proper chew toy and he'll forget about the carpet.

As you are playing with the pup, do not forget to watch him closely and pay attention to his body language. Whenever you see him begin to circle or sniff, take the puppy outside to relieve himself. If you are paper-training, put him back into his confined area on the newspapers. In either case, praise him as he eliminates while he actually is *in the act* of relieving himself. Three seconds after he has finished is too late! You'll be praising him for running toward you, picking up a toy or whatever he may be doing at that moment, and that's not what you want to be praising him for. Timing is a vital tool in all dog training. Use it!

You owe it to your family and your dogs to pick up droppings right away and keep your yard a clean place.

SOMEBODY TO BLAME

House-training a puppy can be frustrating for the puppy and the owner alike. The puppy does not instinctively understand the difference between defecating on the pavement outside and on the ceramic tile in the kitchen. He is confused and frightened by his human's exuberant reactions to his natural urges. The owner, arguably the more intelligent of the duo, is also frustrated that he cannot convince his puppy to obey his commands and instructions.

In frustration, the owner may struggle with the temptation to discipline the puppy, scold him or even strike him on the rear end. Harsh corrections are unnecessary and inappropriate, serving to defeat your purpose in gaining your puppy's trust and respect. Don't blame your nine-week-old puppy. Blame yourself for not being 100% consistent in the puppy's lessons and routine. The lesson here is simple: try harder and your puppy will succeed.

Remove soiled newspapers immediately and replace them with clean ones. You may want to take a small piece of soiled paper and place it in the middle of the new clean papers, as the scent will attract him to that spot when it's time to go again. That scent attraction is why it's so important to clean up any messes made in the house by using a product specially made to eliminate the odor of dog urine and droppings. Regular household cleansers won't do the trick. Pet shops sell the best pet deodorizers. Invest in the largest container you can find.

Scent attraction eventually will lead your pup to his chosen spot outdoors; this is the basis of outdoor training. When you take your puppy outside to relieve himself, use a one-word command such as "Outside" or "Go-potty" (that's one word to the puppy!) as you pick him up and attach his leash. Then put him down in his area. If he is too big for you to carry, snap the leash on quickly and lead him to his spot. Now comes the hard part—hard for you, that is. Just stand there until he urinates and defecates. Move him a few feet in one direction or another if he's just sitting there looking at you, but remember that this is neither playtime nor time for a walk. This is strictly a business trip! Then, as he circles and squats (remember your timing!), give him a quiet "Good dog" as praise. If you start to jump for joy, ecstatic over his performance, he'll do one of two things: either he will stop mid-stream, as it were, or he'll do it again for you—in the house—and expect you to be just as delighted!

Give him five minutes or so and, if he doesn't go in that time, take him back indoors to his confined area and try again in another ten minutes, or immediately if you see him sniffing and circling. By careful observation, you'll soon work out a successful schedule.

Accidents, by the way, are just that—accidents. Clean them up quickly and thoroughly, without

POTTY COMMAND

Most dogs love to please their masters; there are no bounds to what dogs will do to make their owners happy. The potty command is a good example of this theory. If toileting on command makes the master happy, then more power to him. Puppies will obligingly piddle if it really makes their keepers smile. Some owners can be creative about which word they will use to command their dogs to relieve themselves. Some popular choices are "Potty," "Tinkle," "Piddle," "Let's go," "Hurry up" and "Toilet." Give the command every time your puppy goes into position and the puppy will begin to associate his business with the command.

comment, after the puppy has been taken outside to finish his business and then put back into his area or crate. If you witness an accident in progress, say "No!" in a stern voice and get the pup outdoors immediately. No punishment is needed. You and your puppy are just learning each other's language, and sometimes it's easy to miss a puppy's message. Chalk it up to experience and watch more closely from now on.

KEEPING THE PACK ORDERLY

Discipline is a form of training that brings order to life. For example, military discipline is what allows the soldiers in an army to work as one. Discipline is a form of teaching and, in dogs, is the basis of how the successful pack operates. Each member knows his place in the pack and all respect the leader, or alpha dog. It is essential for your puppy that you establish this type of relationship, with you as the alpha, or leader. It is a form of social coexistence that all canines recognize and accept. Discipline, therefore, is never to be confused with punishment. When you teach your puppy how you want

A well-trained Elkhound is a joy to have as a companion who shares your home.

TIPS FOR TRAINING AND SAFETY

1. Whether on or off leash, practice only in a fenced area.
2. Remove the training collar when the training session is over.
3. Don't try to break up a dogfight.
4. "Come," "Leave it" and "Wait" are safety commands.
5. The dog belongs in a crate or behind a barrier when riding in the car.
6. Don't ignore the dog's first sign of aggression. Aggression only gets worse, so take it seriously.
7. Keep the faces of children and dogs separated.
8. Pay attention to what the dog is chewing.
9. Keep the vet's number near your phone.
10. "Okay" is a useful release command.

him to behave, and he behaves properly and you praise him for it, you are disciplining him with a form of positive reinforcement.

For a dog, rewards come in the form of praise, a smile, a cheerful tone of voice, a few friendly pats or a rub of the ears. Rewards are also small food treats. Obviously, that does not mean bits of regular dog food. Instead, treats are very small bits of special things like cheese or pieces of soft dog treats. The idea is to reward the dog with something very small that he can taste and swallow, providing instant positive reinforcement. If he has to take time to chew the treat, he will have forgotten what he did to earn it by the time he is finished!

SMILE WHEN YOU ORDER ME AROUND!

While trainers recommend practicing with your dog every day, it's perfectly acceptable to take a "mental health day" off. It's better not to train the dog on days when you're in a sour mood. Your bad attitude or lack of interest will be sensed by your dog, and he will respond accordingly. Studies show that dogs are well tuned-in to their humans' emotions. Be conscious of how you use your voice when talking to your dog. Raising your voice or shouting will only erode your dog's trust in you as his trainer and master.

You want your Elkhound to look up to you with trust and confidence in all you do together.

Your puppy should never be physically punished. The displeasure shown on your face and in your voice is sufficient to signal to the pup that he has done something wrong. He wants to please everyone higher up on the social ladder, especially his leader, so a scowl and harsh voice will take care of the error. Growling out the word "Shame!" when the pup is caught in the act of doing something wrong is better than the repetitive "No." Some dogs hear "No" so often that they begin to think it's their name! By the way, do not use the dog's name when you're correcting him. His name is reserved to get his attention for something pleasant about to take place.

There are punishments that have nothing to do with you. For example, your dog may think that chasing cats is one reason for his existence. You can try to stop it as much as you like but without

A comfortable collar and a leash with which you can work easily are essential to training your Elkhound.

success because it's such fun for the dog. But one good hissing, spitting, swipe of a cat's claws across the dog's nose will put an end to the game forever. Intervene only when your dog's eyeball is seriously at risk. Cat scratches can cause permanent damage to an innocent but annoying puppy.

PUPPY KINDERGARTEN

Collar and Leash

Before you begin your Norwegian Elkhound puppy's education, he must be used to his collar and leash. Choose a collar for your puppy that is secure, but not heavy or bulky. He won't enjoy training if he's uncomfortable. A buckle collar is fine for everyday wear and for initial puppy training. For older dogs, there are several types of training collars such as the martingale, which is a double loop that tightens slightly around the neck, or the head collar, which is similar to a horse's halter. Do not use a chain choke collar with your Norwegian Elkhound, as it will pull and damage the abundant coat around th dog's neck. Ask your breeder or trainer if and what type of training collar might benefit your adult Elkhound.

A lightweight 6-foot woven cotton or nylon training leash is preferred by most trainers because it is easy to fold up in your hand

WHO'S TRAINING WHOM?

Dog training is a black-and-white exercise. The correct response to a command must be absolute, and the trainer must insist on completely accurate responses from the dog. A trainer cannot command his dog to sit and then settle for the dog's melting into the down position. Often owners are so pleased that their dogs "did something" in response to a command that they just shrug and say, "OK, down" even though they wanted the dog to sit. You want your dog to respond to the command without hesitation: he must respond at that moment and correctly every time.

> **TEACHER'S PET**
> Dogs are individuals, not robots, with many traits basic to their breed. Some, bred to work alone, are independent thinkers; others rely on you to call the shots. If you have enrolled in a training class, your instructor can offer alternative methods of training based on your individual dog's instincts and personality. You may benefit from using a different type of collar or switching to a class with different kinds of dogs.

and comfortable to hold because there is a certain amount of give to it. There are lessons where the dog will start off 6 feet away from you at the end of the leash. The leash used to take the puppy outside to relieve himself is shorter because you don't want him to roam away from his area. The shorter leash will also be the one to use when you walk the puppy.

If you've been wise enough to enroll in a puppy kindergarten training class, suggestions will be made as to the best collar and leash for your young puppy. I say "wise" because your puppy will be in a class with puppies in his age range (up to five months old) of all breeds and sizes. It's the perfect way for him to learn the right way (and the wrong way) to interact with other dogs as well as their people. You cannot teach your puppy how to interpret another dog's sign language. For a first-time puppy owner, these socialization classes are invaluable. For experienced dog owners, they are a real boon to further training.

All training exercises should begin on leash. Only progress to off-leash training in a securely enclosed area and once the command has been learned reliably on leash.

ATTENTION

You've been using the dog's name since the minute you collected him from the breeder, so you should be able to get his attention by saying his name—with a big smile and in an excited tone of

Reclining in the grass is a favorite pastime of many dogs, but most will feel differently when commanded to assume the down position.

voice. His response will be the puppy equivalent of "Here I am! What are we going to do?" Your immediate response (if you haven't guessed by now) is "Good dog." Rewarding him at the moment he pays attention to you teaches him the proper way to respond when he hears his name.

EXERCISES FOR A BASIC CANINE EDUCATION

The Sit Exercise

There are several ways to teach the puppy to sit. The first one is to catch him whenever he is about to sit and, as his backside nears the floor, say "Sit, good dog!" That's positive reinforcement and, if your timing is sharp, he will learn that what he's doing at that second is connected to your saying "Sit" and that you think he's clever for doing it!

Another method is to start with the puppy on his leash in front of you. Show him a treat in the palm of your right hand. Bring your hand up under his nose and, almost in slow motion, move your hand up and back so his nose goes up in the air and his head tilts back as he follows the treat in your hand. At that point, he will have to either sit or fall over, so as his back legs buckle under, say "Sit, good dog," and then give him the treat and lots of praise. You may have to begin with your hand lightly running up his chest,

DON'T STRESS ME OUT

Your dog doesn't have to deal with paying the bills, the daily commute, PTA meetings and the like, but, believe it or not, there's a lot of stress in a dog's world. Stress can be caused by the owner's impatient demeanor and his angry or harsh corrections. If your dog cringes when you reach for his training collar, he's stressed. An older dog is sometimes stressed out when he goes to a new home. No matter what the cause, put off all training until he's over it. If he's going through a fear period—shying away from people, trembling when spoken to, avoiding eye contact or hiding under furniture—wait to resume training. Naturally you'd also postpone your lessons if the dog were sick, and the same goes for you. Show some compassion.

READY, SIT, GO!

On your marks, get set: train! Most professional trainers agree that the sit command is the place to start your dog's formal education. Sitting is a natural posture for most dogs, and they respond to the sit exercise willingly and readily. For every lesson, begin with the sit command so that you start out with a successful exercise; likewise, you should practice the sit command at the end of every lesson as well because you always want to end on a high note.

actually lifting his chin up until he sits. Some (usually older) dogs require gentle pressure on their hindquarters with the left hand, in which case the dog should be on your left side. Puppies generally do not appreciate this physical dominance.

After a few times, you should be able to show the dog a treat in the open palm of your hand, raise your hand waist-high as you say "Sit" and have him sit. Once again, you have taught him two things at the same time. Both the verbal command and the motion of the hand are signals for the sit. Your puppy is watching you almost more than he is listening to you, so what you do is just as important as what you say.

Don't save any of these drills only for training sessions. Use them as much as possible at odd times during a normal day. The dog should always sit before being given his food dish. He should sit to let you go through a doorway first, when the doorbell rings or when you stop to speak to someone on the street.

THE DOWN EXERCISE

Before beginning to teach the down command, you must consider how the dog feels about this exercise. To him, "down" is a submissive position. Being flat on the floor with you standing over him is not his idea of fun. It's up to you to let him know that, while it may not be fun, the reward of your approval is worth his effort.

Start with the puppy on your left side in a sit position. Hold the

The down/stay is a bit more advanced. Begin teaching this command only after he has mastered the basic down command.

SAT IT SIMPLY

When you command your dog to sit, use the word "Sit." Do not say "Sit down," as your dog will not know whether you mean "Sit" or "Down," or maybe you mean both. Be clear in your instructions to your dog; use one-word commands and always be consistent.

leash right above his collar in your left hand. Have an extra-special treat, such as a small piece of cooked chicken or hot dog, in your right hand. Place it at the end of the pup's nose and steadily move your hand down and forward along the ground. Hold the leash to prevent a sudden lunge for the food. As the puppy goes into the down position, say "Down" very gently.

The difficulty with this exercise is twofold: it's both the submissive aspect and the fact that most people say the word "Down" as if they were drill sergeants in charge of recruits! So issue the command sweetly, give him the treat and have the pup maintain the down position for several seconds. If he tries to get up immediately, place your hands on his shoulders and press down gently, giving him a very quiet "Good dog." As you progress with this lesson, increase the "down time" until he will hold it until you say "Okay" (his cue for release). Practice this one in the house at various times throughout the day.

By increasing the length of time during which the dog must maintain the down position, you'll find many uses for it. For example, he can lie at your feet in the vet's office or anywhere that both of you have to wait, when you are on the phone, while the family is eating and so forth. If you progress to training for competitive obedience, he'll already be all set for the exercise called the "long down."

The Stay Exercise

You can teach your Norwegian Elkhound to stay in the sit, down and stand positions. To teach the sit/stay, have the dog sit on your left side. Hold the leash at waist level in your left hand and let the dog know that you have a treat in your closed right hand. Step forward on your right foot as you say "Stay." Immediately turn and stand directly in front of the dog, keeping your right hand up high so he'll keep his eye on the treat hand and maintain the sit position for a count of five. Return to your original position and offer the reward.

Increase the length of the sit/stay each time until the dog can hold it for at least 30 seconds without moving. After about a week of success, move out on your right foot and take two steps before turning to face the dog. Give the "Stay" hand signal (left palm back toward the dog's head) as you leave. He gets the treat when you return and he holds the sit/stay. Increase the distance that you walk away from him before turning until you reach the length of your training leash. But don't rush it! Go back to the beginning if he moves before he should. No matter what the lesson, never be upset by having to back up for a few days. The repetition and practice are what will make your dog reliable in these commands. It won't do any good to move on to something more difficult if the command is not mastered at the easier levels. Above all, even if you do get frustrated, never let your puppy know! Always keep a positive, upbeat attitude during training, which will transmit to your dog for positive results.

OKAY!
This is the signal that tells your dog that he can quit whatever he was doing. Use "Okay" to end a session on a correct response to a command. (Never end on an incorrect response.) Lots of praise follows. People use "Okay" a lot and it has other uses for dogs, too. Your dog is barking. You say, "Okay! Come!" "Okay" signals him to stop the barking activity and "Come" allows him to come to you for a "Good dog."

"Stay" can also be taught in the standing position. The stand/stay is required of show dogs, as they must stand for the judge's examination.

The down/stay is taught in the same way once the dog is completely reliable and steady with the down command. Again, don't rush it. With the dog in the down position on your left side, step out on your right foot as you say "Stay." Return by walking around in back of the dog and into your original position. While you are training, it's okay to murmur something like "Hold on" to encourage him to stay put. When the dog will stay without moving when you are at a distance of 3 or 4 feet, begin to increase the length of time before you return. Be sure he holds the down on your return until you say "Okay." At that point, he gets his treat—just so he'll remember for next time that it's not over until it's over.

COME AND GET IT!

The come command is your dog's safety signal. Until he is 99% perfect in responding, don't use the come command if you cannot enforce it. Practice on leash with treats or squeakers, or whenever the dog is running to you. Never call him to come to you if he is to be corrected for a misdemeanor. Reward the dog with a treat and happy praise whenever he comes to you.

The Come Exercise

No command is more important to the safety of your Norwegian Elkhound than "Come." It is what you should say every single time you see the puppy running toward you: "Thor, come! Good dog." During playtime, run a few feet away from the puppy and turn and tell him to "Come" as he is already running to you. You can go so far as to teach your puppy two things at once if you squat down and hold out your arms. As the pup gets close to you and you're saying "Good dog," bring your right arm in about waist high. Now he's also learning the hand signal, an excellent device should you be on the phone when you need to get him to come to you! You'll also both be one step ahead when you enter obedience classes.

When the puppy responds to your well-timed "Come," try it with the puppy on the training leash. This time, catch him off-guard, while he's sniffing a leaf or watching a bird: "Thor, come!" You may have to pause for a split second after his name to be sure you have his attention. If the puppy shows any sign of confusion, give the leash a mild jerk and take a couple of steps backward. Do not repeat the command. In this case, you should say "Good come" as he reaches you.

That's the number-one rule of training. Each command word is given just once. Anything more is nagging. You'll also notice that all commands are one word only. Even when they are actually two words, you say them as one.

Never call the dog to come to you—with or without his name—if you are angry or intend to correct him for some misbehavior.

When correcting the pup, you go to him. Your dog must always connect "Come" with something pleasant and with your approval; then you can rely on his response. Hound owners know, however, that a reliable come is quite a challenge to teach their curious canines.

Puppies, like children, have notoriously short attention spans, so don't overdo it with any of the training. Keep each lesson short. Break it up with a quick run around the yard or a ball toss, repeat the lesson and quit as soon as the pup gets it right. That way, you will always end with a "Good dog."

Life isn't perfect and neither are puppies. A time will come, often around ten months of age, when he'll become "selectively deaf" or choose to "forget" his name. He may respond by wagging his tail (and even seeming to smile at you) with a look that says "Make me!" Laugh, throw his favorite toy and skip the lesson you had planned. Pups will be pups!

THE HEEL EXERCISE

The second most important command to teach, after the come, is the heel. When you are walking your growing puppy, you need to be in control. Besides, it looks terrible to be pulled and yanked down the street, and it's not much fun either. Your eight- to ten-week-old puppy will probably follow you everywhere, but that's his natural instinct, not your control over the situation. However, any time he does follow you, you can say "Heel" and be ahead of the game, as he will learn to associate this command with the action of following you

LET'S GO!

Many people use "Let's go" instead of "Heel" when teaching their dogs to behave on lead. It sounds more like fun! When beginning to teach the heel, whatever command you use, always step off on your left foot. That's the one next to the dog, who is on your left side, in case you've forgotten. Keep a loose leash. When the dog pulls ahead, stop, bring him back and begin again. Use treats to guide him around turns.

Even the most well-trained of show dogs can be "bribed" with a food reward. This portrait was achieved by focusing the dog's attention on the treat, not the photographer.

before you even begin teaching him to heel.

There is a very precise, almost military, procedure for teaching your dog to heel. As with all other obedience training, begin with the dog on your left side. He will be in a very nice sit and you will have the training leash across your chest. Hold the loop and folded leash in your right hand. Pick up the slack leash above the dog in your left hand and hold it loosely at your side. Step out on your left foot as you say "Heel." If the puppy does not move, give a gentle tug or pat your left leg to get him started. If he surges ahead of you, stop and pull him back gently until he is at your side. Tell him to sit and begin again.

Walk a few steps and stop while the puppy is correctly beside you. Tell him to sit and give mild verbal praise. (More enthusiastic praise will encourage him to think the lesson is over.) Repeat the lesson, increasing the number of steps you take only as long as the dog is heeling nicely beside you. When you end the lesson, have him hold the sit, then give him the "Okay" to let him know that this is the end of the lesson. Praise him so that he knows he did a good job.

The cure for excessive pulling (a common problem) is to stop when the dog is no more than 2 or 3 feet ahead of you. Guide him back into position and begin again. With a really determined puller, try switching to a head collar. When used correctly, this will automatically turn the pup's

BE UPSTANDING!

You are the dog's leader. During training, stand up straight so your dog looks up at you, and therefore up *to* you. Say the command words distinctly, in a clear, declarative tone of voice. (No barking!) Give rewards only as the correct response takes place (remember your timing!). Praise, smiles and treats are "rewards" used to positively reinforce correct responses. Don't repeat a mistake. Just change to another exercise—you will soon find success!

head toward you so you can bring him back easily to the heel position. Give quiet, reassuring praise every time the leash goes slack and he's staying with you.

Staying and heeling can take a lot out of a dog, so provide playtime and free-running exercise to shake off the stress when the lessons are over. You don't want him to associate training with all work and no fun.

TAPERING OFF TIDBITS

Your dog has been watching you—and the hand that treats—throughout all of his lessons, and now it's time to break the treat habit. Begin by giving him treats at the end of each lesson only. Then start to give a treat after the end of only some of the lessons. At the end of every lesson, as well as during the lessons, be consistent with the praise. Your pup now doesn't know whether he'll get a treat or not, but he should keep performing well just in case! Finally, you will stop giving treat rewards entirely. Save them for something brand-new that you want to teach him. Keep up the praise and you'll always have a "good dog."

OBEDIENCE CLASSES

The advantages of an obedience class are that your dog will have to learn amid the distractions of other people and dogs and that your mistakes will be quickly corrected by the trainer. Teaching your dog along with a qualified instructor and other handlers who may have more dog experience than you is another plus of the class environment. The instructor and other handlers can help you to find the most efficient way of teaching your

RIGHT CLICK ON YOUR DOG

With three clicks, the dolphin jumps through the hoop. Wouldn't it be nice to have a dog who could obey wordless commands that easily? Clicker training actually was developed by dolphin trainers and today is used on dogs with great success. You can buy a clicker at a pet shop or pet-supply outlet, and then you'll be off and clicking.

You can click your dog into learning new commands, shaping or conditioning his behavior and solving bad habits. The clicker, used in conjunction with a treat, is an extension of positive reinforcement. The dog begins to recognize your happy clicking, and you will never have to rely on any other method. The dog is conditioned to follow your hand with the clicker, just as he would follow your hand with a treat. To discourage the dog from inappropriate behavior (like jumping up or barking), you can use the clicker to set a timeframe and then click and reward the dog once he's waited the allotted time without jumping up or barking.

dog a command or exercise. It's often easier to learn by other people's mistakes than your own. You will also learn all of the requirements for competitive obedience trials, in which you can earn titles and go on to advanced jumping and retrieving exercises, which are fun for many dogs. Some Elkhounds do basic obedience, but they do require a different type of training than most other dogs. A training class led by someone familiar with the breed is your best bet; ask your breeder for recommendations in your area. Regardless if you go on to compete in obedience or not, obedience classes build the foundation needed for many other canine activities (in which we humans are allowed to participate, too!).

Relaxing for a moment in the ring, the bond between owner and Elkhound is evident. The Elkhound loves any activity that is shared with his favorite person.

TRAINING FOR OTHER ACTIVITIES

Once your dog has basic obedience under his collar and is 12 months of age, you can enter the world of agility training. Many dogs think agility is pure fun, like being turned loose in an amusement park full of obstacles! A Norwegian Elkhound in fit condition can be good at agility, but few set their minds to the task! In Scandinavia, the breed is still used for hunting, but has also been used successfully as a herding dog, specifically on reindeer in Lappland. In the US, people are starting to employ the breed in the herding of sheep and cattle. Some Elkhounds have been used in search-and-rescue work in Scotland and elsewhere. In Norway, the breed is used as a guard dog on farms. The Elkhound also is successfully used as a therapy dog, visiting nursing homes and hospitals. The breed's intelligence seems to let the dog know that he should act gently toward the people he visits.

Around the house, your Norwegian Elkhound can be taught to do some simple chores. You might teach him to carry a small basket of household items or to fetch the morning newspaper. The kids can teach the dog all kinds of tricks, from playing hide-and-seek to balancing a biscuit on his nose. A family dog is what rounds out the family. Everything he does, including sitting at your feet and gazing lovingly at you, represents the bonus of owning a dog.

For young people interested in dog showing, there's nothing better than Junior Showmanship. It's educational, practical, "hands-on" experience, and it's how many successful handlers got their start.

A pair of award-winning Elkhounds. This is a versatile, agile and intelligent breed that is capable of success in many areas of the dog sport.

Physical Structure of the Norwegian Elkhound

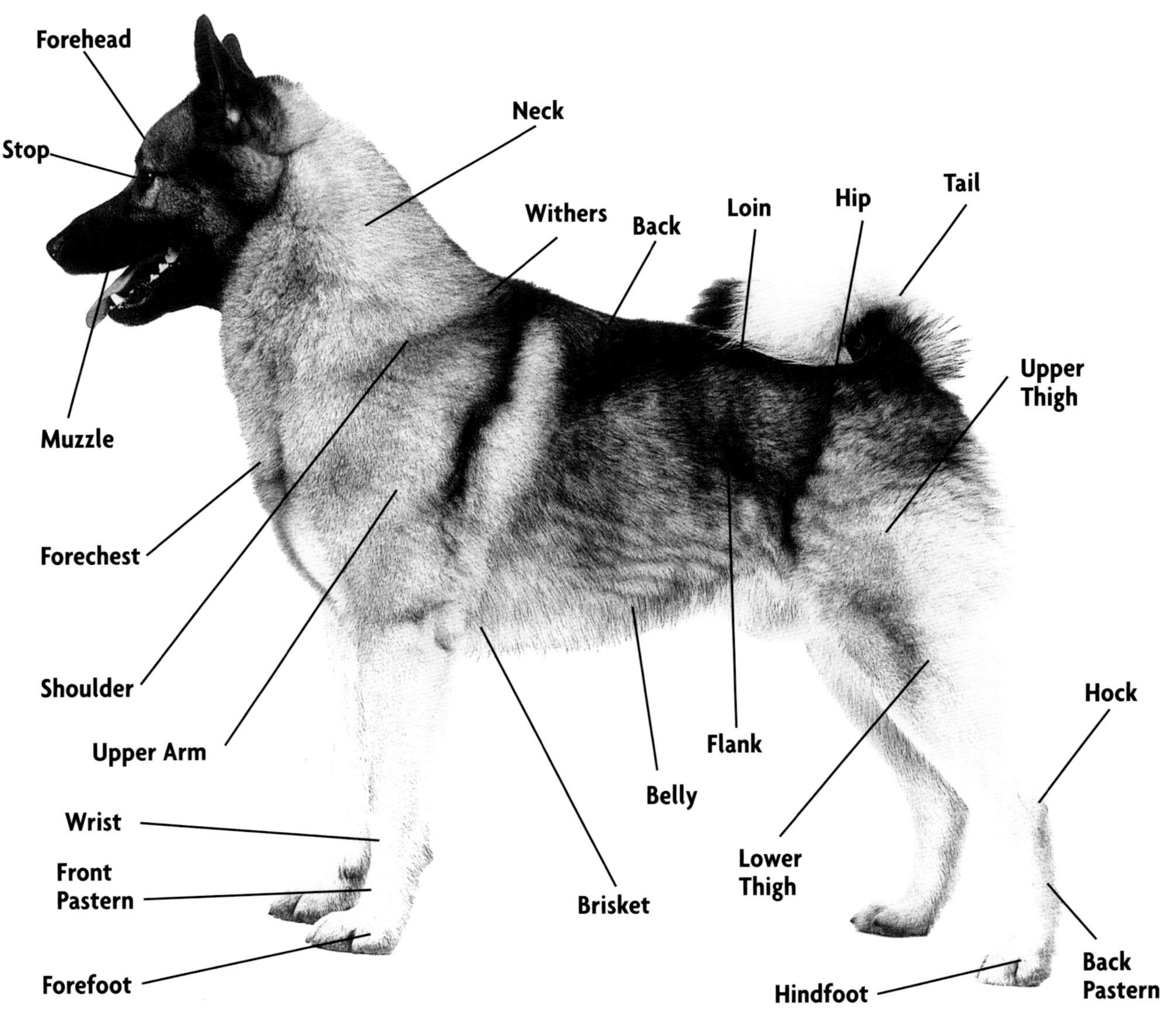

HEALTHCARE OF YOUR
NORWEGIAN ELKHOUND

BY LOWELL ACKERMAN, DVM, DACVD

HEALTHCARE FOR A LIFETIME
When you own a dog, you become his healthcare advocate over his entire lifespan, as well as being the one to shoulder the financial burden of such care. Accordingly, it is worthwhile to focus on prevention rather than treatment, as you and your pet will both be happier.

Of course, the best place to have begun your program of preventive healthcare is with the initial purchase or adoption of your dog. There is no way of guaranteeing that your new furry friend is free of medical problems, but there are some things you can do to improve your odds. You certainly should have done adequate research into the Norwegian Elkhound and have selected your puppy carefully rather than buying on impulse. Health issues aside, a large number of pet abandonment and relinquishment cases arise from a mismatch between pet needs and owner expectations. This is entirely preventable with appropriate planning and finding a good breeder.

Regarding healthcare issues specifically, it is very difficult to make blanket statements about where to acquire a problem-free pet, but, again, a reputable breeder is your best bet. In an ideal situation you have the opportunity to see both parents, get references from other owners of the breeder's pups and see genetic-testing documentation for several generations of the litter's ancestors. At the very least, you must thoroughly investigate your breed of interest and the problems inherent in that breed, as well as the genetic testing available to screen for those problems. Genetic testing offers some important benefits, but testing is available for only a few disorders in a relatively small number of breeds and is not available for some of the most common genetic diseases, such as hip dysplasia, cataracts, epilepsy, cardiomyopathy, etc. This area of research is indeed exciting and increasingly important, and advances will continue to be made each year. In fact, recent research has shown that there is an equivalent dog gene for 75% of known human genes, so research done in either species is likely to benefit the other.

INTERNAL ORGANS OF THE NORWEGIAN ELKHOUND

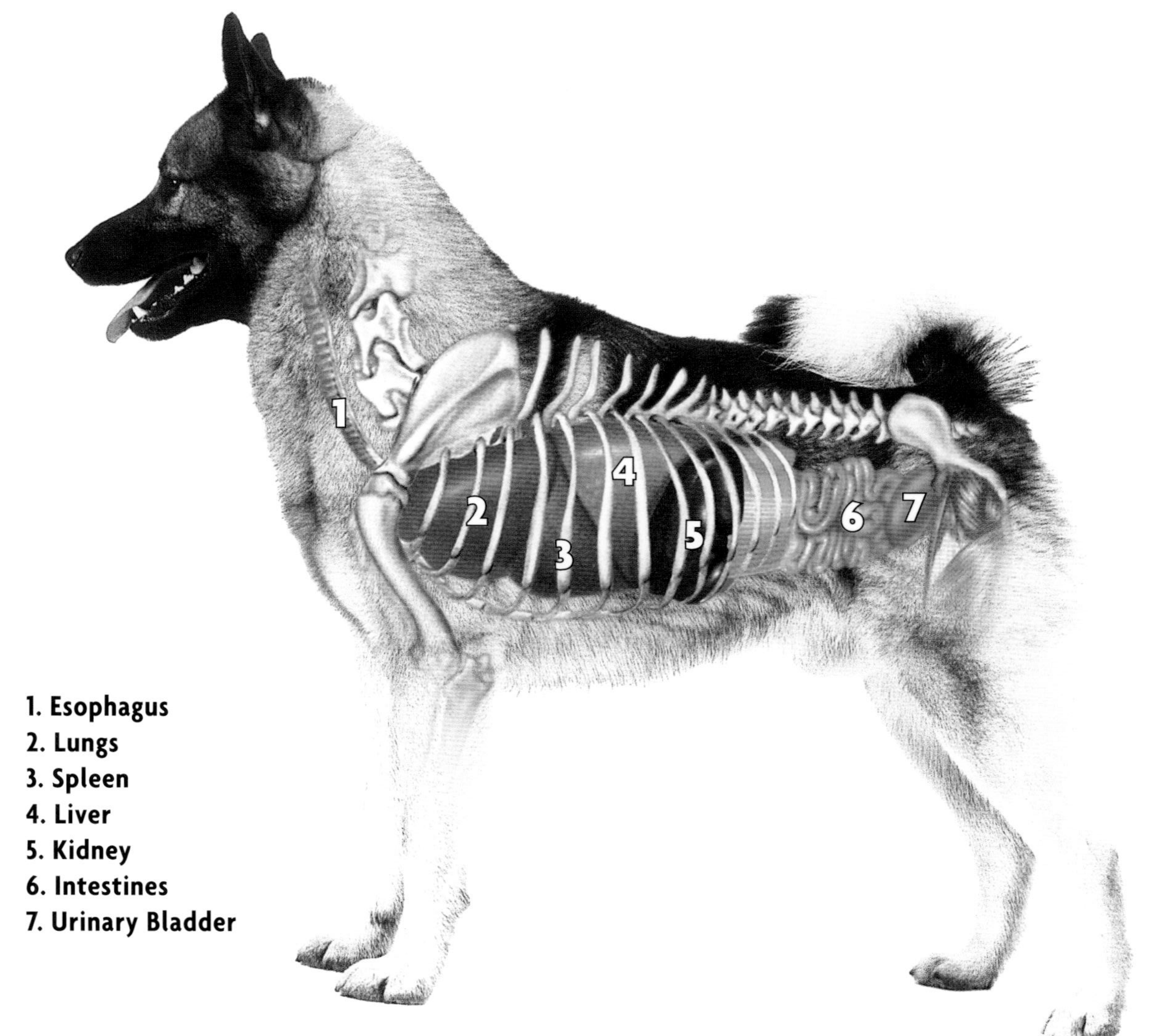

We've also discussed that evaluating the behavioral nature of your Norwegian Elkhound and that of his immediate family members is an important part of the selection process that cannot be underestimated or overemphasized. It is sometimes difficult to evaluate temperament in puppies because certain behavioral tendencies, such as some forms of aggression, may not be immediately evident. More dogs are euthanized each year for behavioral reasons than for all medical conditions combined, so it is critical to take temperament issues seriously. Start with a well-balanced, friendly companion and put the time and effort into proper socialization, and you will both be rewarded with a valued relationship for the life of the dog.

Assuming that you have started off with a pup from healthy, sound stock, you then become responsible for helping your veterinarian keep your pet healthy. Some crucial things happen before you even bring your puppy home. Parasite control typically begins at two weeks of age, and vaccinations typically begin at six to eight weeks of age. A pre-pubertal evaluation is typically scheduled for about six months of age. At this time, a dental evaluation is done (since the adult teeth are now in), heartworm prevention is started and neutering or spaying is most commonly done.

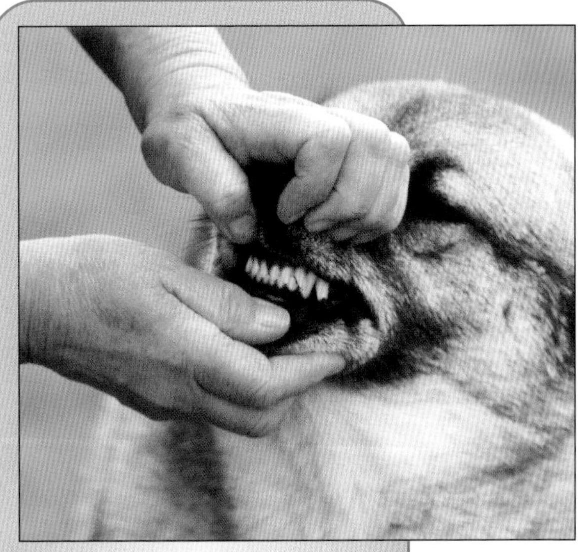

DENTAL WARNING SIGNS

A veterinary dental exam is necessary if you notice one or any combination of the following in your dog:

- Broken, loose or missing teeth
- Loss of appetite (which could be due to mouth pain or illness caused by infection)
- Gum abnormalities, including redness, swelling and bleeding
- Drooling, with or without blood
- Yellowing of the teeth or gumline, indicating tartar
- Bad breath

It is critical to commence regular dental care at home if you have not already done so. It may not sound very important, but most dogs have active periodontal disease by four years of age if they don't have their teeth cleaned regu-

Skeletal Structure of the Norwegian Elkhound

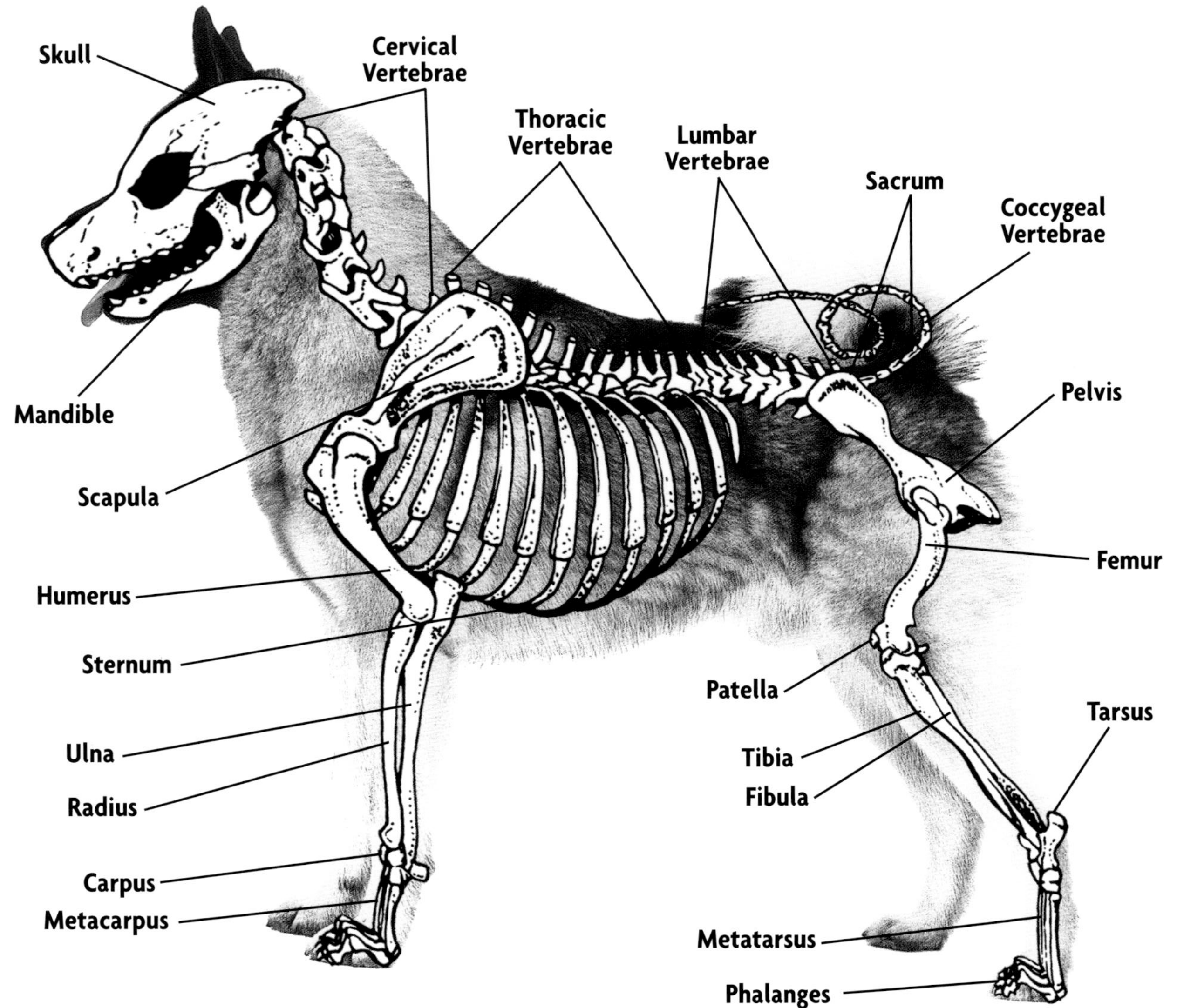

larly at home, not just at their veterinary exams. Dental problems lead to more than just bad "doggy breath." Gum disease can have very serious medical consequences. If you start brushing your dog's teeth and using antiseptic rinses from a young age, your dog will be accustomed to it and will not resist. The results will be healthy dentition, which your pet will need to enjoy a long, healthy life.

Most dogs are considered adults at a year of age, although most breeds continue filling out until about two or so years old. Even individual dogs within each breed have different healthcare requirements, so work with your veterinarian to determine what will be needed and what your role should be. This doctor-client relationship is important because as vaccination guidelines change, there may not be an annual "vaccine visit" scheduled. You must make sure that you see your veterinarian at least annually, even if no vaccines are due, because this is the best opportunity to coordinate healthcare activities and to make sure that no medical issues creep by unaddressed.

When your Norwegian Elkhound reaches three-quarters of his anticipated lifespan, he is considered a "senior" and will

Don't Eat the Daisies!

Many plants and flowers are beautiful to look at, but can be highly toxic if ingested by your dog. Reactions range from abdominal pain and vomiting to convulsions and death. If the following plants are in your home, remove them. If they are outside your house or in your garden, avoid accidents by removing them or making sure your dog is never left unsupervised in those locations.

Azalea
Belladonna
Bird of paradise
Bulbs
Calla lily
Cardinal flower
Castor bean
Chinaberry tree
Daphne
Dumb cane
Dutchman's breeches
Elephant's ear
Hydrangea
Jack-in-the-pulpit
Jasmine
Jimsonweed
Larkspur
Laurel
Lily of the valley
Mescal bean
Mushrooms
Nightshade
Philodendron
Poinsettia
Prunus species
Tobacco
Yellow jasmine
Yews, *Taxus* species

YOUR DOG NEEDS TO VISIT THE VET IF:

- He has ingested a toxin such as antifreeze or a toxic plant; in these cases, administer first aid and call the vet right away
- His teeth are discolored, loose or missing or he has sores or other signs of infection or abnormality in the mouth
- He has been vomiting, has had diarrhea or has been constipated for over 24 hours; call immediately if you notice blood
- He has refused food for over 24 hours
- His eating habits, water intake or toilet habits have noticeably changed; if you have noticed weight gain or weight loss
- He shows symptoms of bloat, which requires *immediate* attention
- He is salivating excessively
- He has a lump in his throat
- He has a lump or bumps anywhere on the body
- He is very lethargic
- He appears to be in pain or otherwise has trouble chewing or swallowing
- His skin loses elasticity

Of course, there will be other instances in which a visit to the vet is necessary; these are just some of the signs that could be indicative of serious problems that need to be caught as early as possible.

require some special attention to his health. In general, if you've been taking great care of your canine companion throughout his formative and adult years, the transition to senior status should be a smooth one. Age is not a disease, and as long as everything is functioning as it should, there is no reason why most of late adulthood should not be rewarding for both you and your pet. This is especially true if you have tended to the details, such as regular veterinary visits, proper dental care, excellent nutrition and management of bone and joint issues.

At this stage in your Norwegian Elkhound's life, your veterinarian should want to schedule visits twice yearly, instead of once, to run some laboratory screenings, electrocardiograms and the like, and to change the diet to something more digestible. Catching problems early is the best way to manage them effectively. Treating the early stages of heart disease is so much easier than trying to intervene when there is more significant damage to the heart muscle. Similarly, managing the beginning of kidney problems is fairly routine if there is no significant kidney damage. Other problems, like cognitive dysfunction (similar to senility and Alzheimer's disease), cancer, diabetes and arthritis, are more common in older dogs, but all can be treated to help the dog live as many happy, comfortable years as possible. Just as in people, medical management is more effective (and less expensive) when you catch things early.

SELECTING A VETERINARIAN

There is probably no more important decision that you will make regarding your pet's healthcare than the selection of his doctor. Your pet's veterinarian will be a pediatrician, family-practice physician and gerontologist, depending on the dog's life stage, and will be the individual who makes recommendations regarding issues such as when specialists need to be consulted, when diagnostic testing and/or therapeutic intervention is needed and when you will need to seek outside emergency and critical-care services. Your vet will act as your advocate and liaison throughout these processes.

Everyone has his own idea about what to look for in a vet, an individual who will play a big role in his dog's (and, of course, his own) life for many years to come. For some, it is the compassionate caregiver with whom they hope to develop a professional relationship to span the lifetime of their dogs and even their future pets. For others, they are seeking a clinician with keen diagnostic and therapeutic insight who can deliver state-of-the-art healthcare. Still others need a veterinary facility that is open evenings and weekends, is in close proximity or provides mobile veterinary services to accommodate their schedules; these people may not much mind that their dogs might see different veterinarians on each visit. Just as we have different reasons for selecting our own healthcare professionals (e.g., covered by

TAKING YOUR DOG'S TEMPERATURE

It is important to know how to take your dog's temperature at times when you think he may be ill. It's not the most enjoyable task, but it can be done without too much difficulty. It's easier with a helper, preferably someone with whom the dog is friendly, so that one of you can hold the dog while the other inserts the thermometer.

Before inserting the thermometer, coat the end with petroleum jelly. Insert the thermometer slowly and gently into the dog's rectum about one inch. Wait for the reading, about two minutes. Be sure to remove the thermometer carefully and clean it thoroughly after each use.

A dog's normal body temperature is between 100.5 and 102.5 degrees F. Immediate veterinary attention is required if the dog's temperature is below 99 or above 104 degrees F.

insurance plan, expert in field, convenient location, etc.), we should not expect that there is a one-size-fits-all recommendation for selecting a veterinarian and veterinary practice. The best advice is to be honest in your assessment of what you expect from a veterinary practice and to conscientiously research the options in your area. You will quickly appreciate that not all veterinary practices are the same, and you will be happiest with one that truly meets your needs.

There is another point to be considered in the selection of veterinary services. Not that long ago, a single veterinarian would attempt to manage all medical and surgical issues as they arose. That was often problematic because veterinarians are trained in many species and many diseases, and it was just impossible for general veterinary practitioners to be experts in every species, every breed, every field and every ailment. However, just as in the human healthcare fields, specialization has allowed general practitioners to concentrate on primary healthcare delivery, especially wellness and the prevention of infectious diseases, and to utilize a network of specialists to assist in the management of conditions that require specific expertise and experience. Thus there are now many types of veterinary specialists, including dermatologists, cardiologists, ophthalmologists, surgeons, internists, oncologists, neurologists, behaviorists, criticalists and others to help primary-care veterinarians deal with complicated medical challenges. In most cases, specialists see cases referred by primary-care veterinarians, make diagnoses and set up management plans. From there, the animals' ongoing care is returned to their primary-care veterinarians. This important team approach to your pet's medical-care needs has provided opportunities for advanced care and an unparalleled level of quality to be delivered.

With all of the opportunities for your Norwegian Elkhound to receive high-quality veterinary medical care, there is another topic that needs to be addressed at the same time—cost. It's been said that you can have excellent healthcare or inexpensive healthcare, but never both; this is as true in veterinary medicine as it is in human medicine. While veterinary costs are a fraction of what the same services cost in the human healthcare arena, it is still difficult to deal with unanticipated medical costs, especially since they can easily creep into hundreds or even thousands of dollars if specialists or emergency services become involved. However, there are ways of managing these risks. The easiest is to buy pet health insurance and

PROBLEM: AND THAT STARTS WITH "P"

Urinary tract problems more commonly affect female dogs, especially those who have been spayed. The first sign that a urinary tract problem exists usually is a strong odor from the urine or an unusual color. Blood in the urine, known as hematuria, is another sign of an infection, related to cystitis, a bladder infection, bladder cancer or a blood-clotting disorder. Urinary tract problems can also be signaled by the dog's straining while urinating, experiencing pain during urination and genital discharge as well as excessive water intake and urination.

Excessive drinking, in and of itself, does not indicate a urinary tract problem. A dog who is drinking more than normal may have a kidney or liver problem, a hormonal disorder or diabetes mellitus. Behaviorists report a disorder known as psychogenic polydipsia, which manifests itself in excessive drinking and urination. If you notice your dog drinking much more than normal, take him to the vet.

realize that its foremost purpose is not to cover routine healthcare visits but rather to serve as an umbrella for those rainy days when your pet needs medical care and you don't want to worry about whether or not you can afford that care.

Pet insurance policies are very cost-effective (and very inexpensive by human health-insurance standards), but make sure that you buy the policy long before you intend to use it (preferably starting in puppyhood because coverage will exclude pre-existing conditions) and that you are actually buying an indemnity insurance plan from an insurance company that is regulated by your state or province. Many insurance policy look-alikes are actually discount clubs that are redeemable only at specific locations and

Elkhounds, being natural hunters, love to explore the great outdoors—and much of the great outdoors can get trapped in the Elkhound's heavy coat. Examine your dog's skin and coat regularly, especially after time spent outdoors.

for specific services. An indemnity plan covers your pet at almost all veterinary, specialty and emergency practices and is an excellent way to manage your pet's ongoing healthcare needs.

VACCINATIONS AND INFECTIOUS DISEASES

There has never been an easier time to prevent a variety of infectious diseases in your dog, but the advances we've made in veterinary medicine come with a price—choice. Now while choice regarding vaccinations may seem like a good thing, and it is, it also has never been more difficult for the pet owner (or the veterinarian) to make an informed decision about the best way to protect pets through vaccination.

Years ago, it was just accepted that puppies got a starter series of vaccinations and then annual "boosters" throughout their lives to keep them protected. As more and more vaccines became available, consumers wanted the convenience of having all of that protection in a single injection. The result was "multivalent" vaccines that crammed a lot of protection into a single syringe. The manufacturers' recommendations were to give the vaccines

FOOD ALLERGY

Severe itching, leading to bald patches and open sores on the feet, face, ears, armpits and groin, could be caused by a food allergy. Studies indicate that up to 10% of dogs suffer from food allergies, which develop slowly over time without a change in diet. Dogs who suffer from chronic ear problems may actually have a food allergy. Unfortunately, there are no tests available to determine whether your dog definitely suffers from a food allergy. The dog will be miserable and you will be frustrated and stressed.

Take the problem into your own hands and kitchen. Select a type of meat that your dog is not getting from his existing diet, perhaps white fish, lamb or venison, and prepare a home-cooked food. The food should consist of two parts carbohydrate (rice, pasta or potatoes) and one part protein (the chosen meat). It's better not to start with soy as the protein source unless all of the meats cause a reaction.

Monitor your dog's intake carefully. He must eat only your prepared meal without any treats or side-trips to the garbage can. All family members (and visiting friends) must be informed of the plan. After four or five weeks on the new diet, you will reintroduce a portion of his original diet to determine whether this food is the cause of the skin irritation (or other reactions). Once the dog reacts to the change in diet, resume the new diet. Make dietary modifications every two weeks and keep careful records of any reactions the dog has to the diet.

Common Infectious Diseases

Let's discuss some of the diseases that create the need for vaccination in the first place. Following are the major canine infectious diseases and a simple explanation of each.

Rabies: A devastating viral disease that can be fatal in dogs and people. In fact, vaccination of dogs and cats is an important public-health measure to create a resistant animal buffer population to protect people from contracting the disease. Vaccination schedules are determined on a government level and are not optional for pet owners; rabies vaccination is required by law in all 50 states.

Parvovirus: A severe, potentially life-threatening disease that is easily transmitted between dogs. There are four strains of the virus, but it is believed that there is significant "cross-protection" between strains that may be included in individual vaccines.

Distemper: A potentially severe and life-threatening disease with a relatively high risk of exposure, especially in certain regions. In very high-risk distemper environments, young pups may be vaccinated with human measles vaccine, a related virus that offers cross-protection when administered at four to ten weeks of age.

Hepatitis: Caused by canine adenovirus type 1 (CAV-1), but since vaccination with the causative virus has a higher rate of adverse effects, cross-protection is derived from the use of adenovirus type 2 (CAV-2), a cause of respiratory disease and one of the potential causes of canine cough. Vaccination with CAV-2 provides long-term immunity against hepatitis, but relatively less protection against respiratory infection.

Canine cough: Also called tracheobronchitis, actually a fairly complicated result of viral and bacterial offenders; therefore, even with vaccination, protection is incomplete. Wherever dogs congregate, canine cough will likely be spread among them. Intranasal vaccination with *Bordetella* and parainfluenza is the best safeguard, but the duration of immunity does not appear to be very long, typically a year at most. These are non-core vaccines, but vaccination is sometimes mandated by boarding kennels, obedience classes, dog shows and other places where dogs congregate to try to minimize spread of infection.

Leptospirosis: A potentially fatal disease that is more common in some geographic regions. It is capable of being spread to humans. The disease varies with the individual "serovar," or strain, of *Leptospira* involved. Since there does not appear to be much cross-protection between serovars, protection is only as good as the likelihood that the serovar in the vaccine is the same as the one in the pet's local environment. Problems with *Leptospira* vaccines are that protection does not last very long, side effects are not uncommon and a large percentage of dogs (perhaps 30%) may not respond to vaccination.

Borrelia burgdorferi: The cause of Lyme disease, the risk of which varies with the geographic area in which the pet lives and travels. Lyme disease is spread by deer ticks in the eastern US and western black-legged ticks in the western part of the country, and the risk of exposure is high in some regions. Lameness, fever and inappetence are most commonly seen in affected dogs. The extent of protection from the vaccine has not been conclusively demonstrated.

Coronavirus: This disease has a high risk of exposure, especially in areas where dogs congregate, but it typically causes only mild to moderate digestive upset (diarrhea, vomiting, etc.). Vaccines are available, but the duration of protection is believed to be relatively short and the effectiveness of the vaccine in preventing infection is considered low.

There are many other vaccinations available, including those for *Giardia* and canine adenovirus-1. While there may be some specific indications for their use, and local risk factors to be considered, they are not widely recommended for most dogs.

annually, and this was a simple enough protocol to follow. However, as veterinary medicine has become more sophisticated and we have started looking more at healthcare quandaries rather than convenience, it became necessary to reevaluate the situation and deal with some tough questions. It is important to realize that whether or not to use a particular vaccine depends on the risk of contracting the disease against which it protects, the severity of the disease if it is contracted, the duration of immunity provided by the vaccine, the safety of the product and the needs of the individual animal. In a very general sense, rabies, distemper, hepatitis and parvovirus are considered core vaccine needs, while parainfluenza, *Bordetella bronchiseptica*, leptospirosis, coronavirus and borreliosis (Lyme disease) are considered non-core needs and best reserved for animals that demonstrate reasonable risk of contracting the diseases.

NEUTERING/SPAYING

Sterilization procedures (neutering for males/spaying for females) are meant to accomplish several purposes. While the underlying premise is to address the risk of pet overpopulation, there are also some medical and behavioral benefits to the surgeries. For females, spaying prior to the first estrus (heat cycle) leads to a marked reduction in the risk of mammary cancer and other female health problems. There also will be no manifestations of "heat" to attract male dogs and no bleeding in the house. For males, there is prevention of testicular cancer and a reduction in the risk of prostate problems. In both sexes there may be some limited reduction in aggressive behaviors toward other dogs, and some diminishing of urine marking, roaming and mounting.

While neutering and spaying do indeed prevent animals from contributing to pet overpopulation, even no-cost and low-cost neutering options have not eliminated the problem. Perhaps one of the main reasons for this is that individuals that intentionally breed their dogs and those that allow their animals to run at large are the main causes of unwanted offspring. Also, animals in shelters are often there because they were abandoned or relinquished, not because they came from unplanned matings. Neutering/spaying is important, but it should be considered in the context of the real causes of animals' ending up in shelters and eventually being euthanized.

One of the important considerations regarding neutering is that it is a surgical procedure.

This sometimes gets lost in discussions of low-cost procedures and commoditization of the process. In females, spaying is specifically referred to as an ovariohysterectomy. In this procedure, a midline incision is made in the abdomen and the entire uterus and both ovaries are surgically removed. While this is a major invasive surgical procedure, it usually has few complications because it is typically performed on healthy young animals. However, it is major surgery, as any woman who has had a hysterectomy will attest.

In males, neutering has traditionally referred to castration, which involves the surgical removal of both testicles. While still a significant piece of surgery, there is not the abdominal exposure that is required in the female surgery. In addition, there is now a chemical sterilization option, in which a solution is injected into each testicle, leading to atrophy of the sperm-producing cells. This can typically be done under sedation rather than full anesthesia. This is a relatively new approach, and there are no long-term clinical studies yet available.

Neutering/spaying is typically done around six months of age at most veterinary hospitals, although techniques have been pioneered to perform the procedures in animals as young as eight weeks of age. In general, the surgeries on the very young animals are done for the specific reason of sterilizing them before they go to their new homes. This is done in some shelter hospitals for assurance that the animals will definitely not produce any pups. Otherwise, these organizations need to rely on owners to comply with their wishes to have the animals "altered" at a later date, something that does not always happen.

Still in great shape at the amazing age of 15, Ch. Kensix Trojan is a testament to longevity and hardiness in the Norwegian Elkhound breed.

S. E. M. by Dr. Dennis Kunkel, University of Hawaii.

A scanning electron micrograph of a dog flea, *Ctenocephalides canis*, on dog hair.

EXTERNAL PARASITES

Fleas

Fleas have been around for millions of years and, while we have better tools now for controlling them than at any time in the past, there still is little chance that they will end up on an endangered species list. Actually, they are very well adapted to living on our pets, and they continue to adapt as we make advances.

The female flea can consume 15 times her weight in blood during active reproduction and can lay as many as 40 eggs a day. These eggs are very resistant to the effects of insecticides. They hatch into larvae, which then mature and spin cocoons. The immature fleas reside in this pupal stage until the time is right for feeding. This pupal stage is also very resistant to the effects of insecticides, and pupae can last in the environment without feeding for many months. Newly emergent fleas are attracted to animals by the warmth of the animals' bodies, movement and exhaled carbon dioxide. However, when they first emerge from their cocoons, they orient towards light; thus when an animal passes between a flea and the light source, casting a shadow, the flea pounces and starts to feed. If the animal turns out to be a dog or cat, the reproductive cycle continues. If the flea lands on another type of animal, including a person, the flea will bite but will then look for a more appropriate host. An emerging adult flea can survive without feeding for up to 12 months but, once it tastes blood, it can survive off its host for only three to four days.

It was once thought that fleas spend most of their lives in the environment, but we now know that fleas won't willingly jump off a dog unless leaping to another dog or when physically removed by brushing, bathing or other manipulation. Flea eggs, on the other hand, are shiny and smooth, and they roll off the animal and into the environment. The eggs, larvae and pupae then exist in the environment, but once the adult finds a susceptible animal, it's home sweet home until the flea is forced to seek refuge elsewhere.

Since adult fleas live on the animal and immature forms survive in the environment, a successful treatment plan must address all stages of the flea life cycle. There are now several safe and effective flea-control products that can be applied on a monthly basis. These include fipronil, imidacloprid, selamectin and permethrin (found in several formulations). Most of these products have significant flea-killing rates within 24 hours. However, none of them will control the immature forms in the environment. To accomplish this, there are a variety of insect growth regulators that can be sprayed into

FLEA PREVENTION FOR YOUR DOG

- Discuss with your veterinarian the safest product to protect your dog, likely in the form of a monthly tablet or a liquid preparation placed on the back of the dog's neck.
- For dogs suffering from flea-bite dermatitis, a shampoo or topical insecticide treatment is required.
- Your lawn and property should be sprayed with an insecticide designed to kill fleas and ticks that lurk outdoors.
- Using a flea comb, check the dog's coat regularly for any signs of parasites.
- Practice good housekeeping. Vacuum floors, carpets and furniture regularly, especially in the areas that the dog frequents, and wash the dog's bedding weekly.
- Follow up house-cleaning with carpet shampoos and sprays to rid the house of fleas at all stages of development. Insect growth regulators are the safest option.

THE FLEA'S LIFE CYCLE

What came first, the flea or the egg? This age-old mystery is more difficult to comprehend than the actual cycle of the flea. Fleas usually live only about four months. A female can lay 2,000 eggs in her lifetime.

Photo by Carolina Biological Supply Co.

Egg

After ten days of rolling around your carpet or under your furniture, the eggs hatch into larvae, which feed on various and sundry debris. In days or months, depending on the climate, the larvae spin cocoons and develop into the pupal or nymph stage, which quickly develop into fleas.

Larva

Photo by Carolina Biological Supply Co.

Pupa

These immature fleas must locate a host within 10 to 14 days or they will die. Only about 1% of the flea population exist as adult fleas, while the other 99% exist as eggs, larvae or pupae.

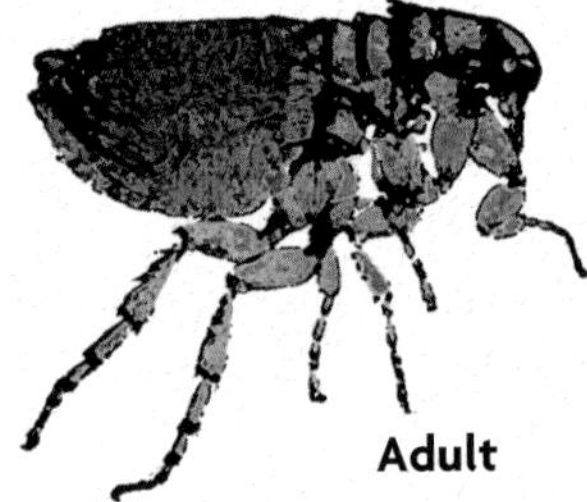

Adult

KILL FLEAS THE NATURAL WAY

If you choose not to go the route of conventional medication, there are some natural ways to ward off fleas:

- Dust your dog with a natural flea powder, composed of such herbal goodies as rosemary, wormwood, pennyroyal, citronella, rue, tobacco powder and eucalyptus.
- Apply diatomaceous earth, the fossilized remains of single-cell algae, to your carpets, furniture and pet's bedding. Even though it's not good for dogs, it's even worse for fleas, which will dry up swiftly and die.
- Brush your dog frequently, give him adequate exercise and let him fast occasionally. All of these activities strengthen the dog's system and make him more resistant to disease and parasites.
- Bathe your dog with a capful of pennyroyal or eucalyptus oil.
- Feed a natural diet, free of additives and preservatives. Add some fresh garlic and brewer's yeast to the dog's morning portion, as these items have flea-repelling properties.

the environment (e.g., pyriproxyfen, methoprene, fenoxycarb) as well as insect development inhibitors such as lufenuron that can be administered. These compounds have no effect on adult fleas, but they stop immature forms from developing into adults. In years gone by, we relied heavily on toxic insecticides (such as organophosphates, organochlorines and carbamates) to manage the flea problem, but today's options are not only much safer to use on our pets but also safer for the environment.

TICKS

Ticks are members of the spider class (arachnids) and are blood-sucking parasites capable of transmitting a variety of diseases, including Lyme disease, ehrlichiosis, babesiosis and Rocky Mountain spotted fever. It's easy to see ticks on your own skin, but it is more of a challenge when your furry companion is affected. Whenever you happen to be planning a stroll in a tick-infested area (especially forests, grassy or wooded areas or parks) be prepared to do a thorough inspection of your dog afterward to search for ticks. Ticks can be tricky, so make sure you spend time looking in the ears, between the toes and everywhere else where a tick might hide. Ticks need to be attached for 24–72 hours before they transmit most of the diseases that they carry, so you do have a window of opportunity for some preventive intervention.

S. E. M. BY PHOTOTAKE.

A scanning electron micrograph of the head of a female deer tick, *Ixodes dammini*, a parasitic tick that carries Lyme disease.

Female ticks live to eat and breed. They can lay between 4,000 and 5,000 eggs and they die soon after. Males, on the other hand, live only to mate with the females and continue the process as long as they are able. Most ticks live on multiple hosts before parasitizing dogs. The immature forms typically reside on grass and shrubs, waiting for susceptible animals to walk by. The larvae and nymph stages typically feed on wildlife.

If only a few ticks are present on a dog, they can be plucked out, but it is important to remove the entire head and mouthparts,

A TICKING BOMB

There is nothing good about a tick's harpooning his nose into your dog's skin. Among the diseases caused by ticks are Rocky Mountain spotted fever, canine ehrlichiosis, canine babesiosis, canine hepatozoonosis and Lyme disease. If a dog is allergic to the saliva of a female wood tick, he can develop tick paralysis.

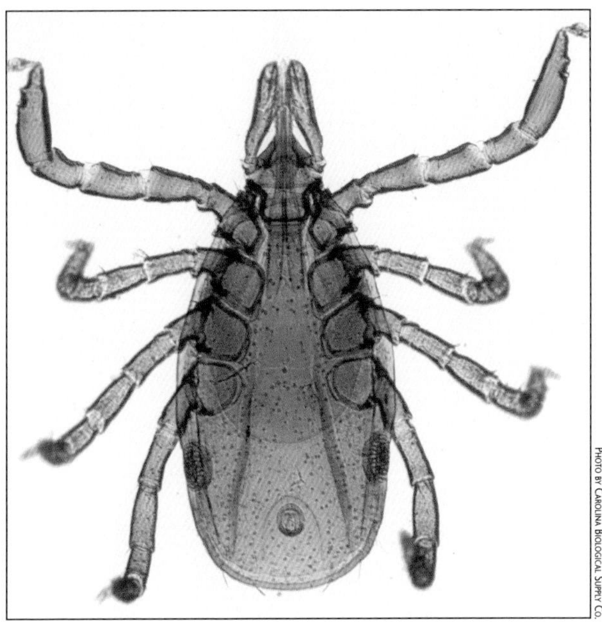
Photo by Carolina Biological Supply Co.

Deer tick, *Ixodes dammini*.

which may be deeply embedded in the skin. This is best accomplished with forceps designed especially for this purpose; fingers can be used but should be protected with rubber gloves, plastic wrap or at least a paper towel. The tick should be grasped as closely as possible to the animal's skin and should be pulled upward with steady, even pressure. Do not squeeze, crush or puncture the body of the tick or you risk exposure to any disease carried by that tick. Once the ticks have been removed, the sites of attachment should be disinfected. Your hands should then be washed with soap and water to further minimize risk of contagion. The tick should be disposed of in a container of alcohol or household bleach.

Some of the newer flea products, specifically those with fipronil, selamectin and permethrin, have effect against some, but not all, species of tick. Flea collars containing appropriate pesticides (e.g., propoxur, chlorfenvinphos) can aid in tick control. In most areas, such collars should be placed on animals in March, at the beginning of the tick season, and changed regularly. Leaving the collar on when the pesticide level is waning invites the development of resistance. Amitraz collars are also good for tick control, and the active ingredient does not interfere with other flea-control products. The ingredient helps prevent the attachment of ticks to the skin and will cause those ticks already on the skin to detach themselves.

TICK CONTROL

Removal of underbrush and leaf litter and the thinning of trees in areas where tick control is desired are recommended. These actions remove the cover and food sources for small animals that serve as hosts for ticks. With continued mowing of grasses in these areas, the probability of ticks' surviving is further reduced. A variety of insecticide ingredients (e.g., resmethrin, carbaryl, permethrin, chlorpyrifos, dioxathion and allethrin) are registered for tick control around the home.

Mites

Mites are tiny arachnid parasites that parasitize the skin of dogs. Skin diseases caused by mites are referred to as "mange," and there are many different forms seen in dogs. These forms are very different from one another, each one warranting an individual description.

Sarcoptic mange, or scabies, is one of the itchiest conditions that affects dogs. The microscopic *Sarcoptes* mites burrow into the superficial layers of the skin and can drive dogs crazy with itchiness. They are also communicable to people, although they can't complete their reproductive cycle on people. In addition to being tiny, the mites also are often difficult to find when trying to make a diagnosis. Skin scrapings from multiple areas are examined microscopically but, even then, sometimes the mites cannot be found.

Fortunately, scabies is relatively easy to treat, and there are a variety of products that will successfully kill the mites. Since the mites can't live in the environment for very long without feeding, a complete cure is usually possible within four to eight weeks.

Cheyletiellosis is caused by a relatively large mite, which sometimes can be seen even without a microscope. Often referred to as "walking dandruff," this also causes itching, but not usually as profound as with scabies. While *Cheyletiella* mites can survive somewhat longer in the environment than scabies mites, they too are relatively easy to treat, being responsive to not only the medications used to treat scabies but also often to flea-control products.

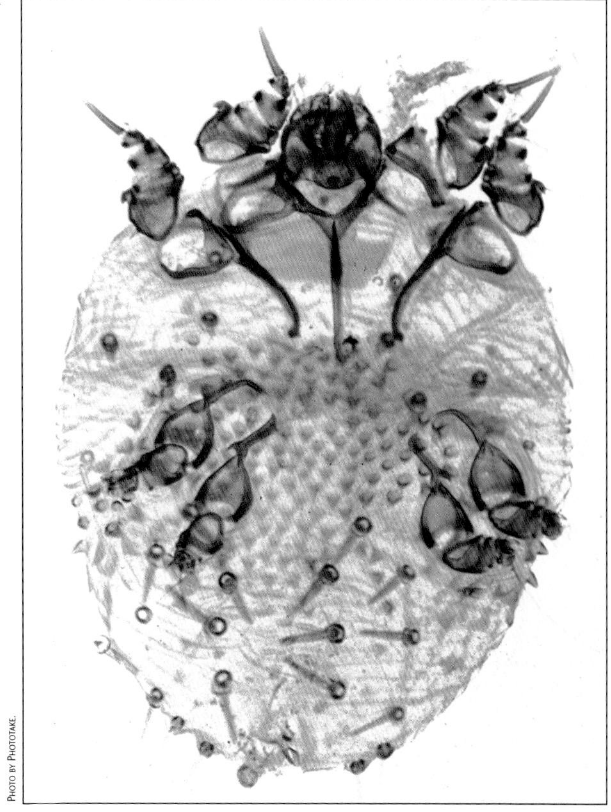

Photo by Phototake.

***Sarcoptes scabiei*, commonly known as the "itch mite."**

Otodectes cynotis is the canine ear mite and is one of the more common causes of mange, especially in young dogs in shelters or pet stores. That's because the mites are typically present in large numbers and are quickly spread to nearby animals. The mites rarely do

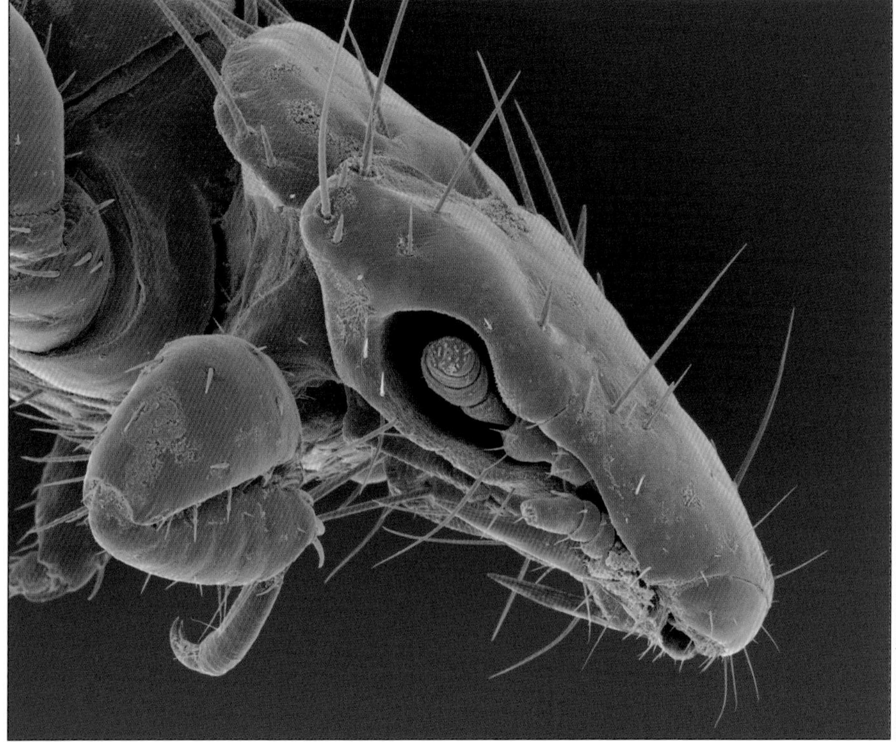

Micrograph of a dog louse, *Heterodoxus spiniger*. Female lice attach their eggs to the hairs of the dog. As the eggs hatch, the larval lice bite and feed on the blood. Lice can also feed on dead skin and hair. This feeding activity can cause hair loss and skin problems.

S. E. M. by Dr. Dennis Kunkel, University of Hawaii.

much harm but can be difficult to eradicate if the treatment regimen is not comprehensive. While many try to treat the condition with ear drops only, this is the most common cause of treatment failure. Ear drops cause the mites to simply move out of the ears and as far away as possible (usually to the base of the tail) until the insecticide levels in the ears drop to an acceptable level—then it's back to business as usual! The successful treatment of ear mites requires treating all animals in the household with a systemic insecticide, such as selamectin, or a combination of miticidal ear drops combined with whole-body flea-control preparations.

Demodicosis, sometimes referred to as red mange, can be one of the most difficult forms of mange to treat. Part of the problem has to do with the fact that the mites live in the hair follicles and they are relatively well shielded from topical and systemic products. The main issue, however, is that demodectic mange typically results only when there is some underlying process interfering with the dog's immune system.

Since *Demodex* mites are normal residents of the skin of

mammals, including humans, there is usually a mite population explosion only when the immune system fails to keep the number of mites in check. In young animals, the immune deficit may be transient or may reflect an actual inherited immune problem. In older animals, demodicosis is usually seen only when there is another disease hampering the immune system, such as diabetes, cancer, thyroid problems or the use of immune-suppressing drugs. Accordingly, treatment involves not only trying to kill the mange mites but also discerning what is interfering with immune function and correcting it if possible.

ILLUSTRATION BY PHOTOTAKE.

Illustration of *Demodex folliculoram.*

Chiggers represent several different species of mite that don't parasitize dogs specifically, but do latch on to passersby and can cause irritation. The problem is most prevalent in wooded areas in the late summer and fall. Treatment is not difficult, as the mites do not complete their life cycle on dogs and are susceptible to a variety of miticidal products.

MOSQUITOES

Mosquitoes have long been known to transmit a variety of diseases to people, as well as just being biting pests during warm weather. They also pose a real risk to pets. Not only do they carry deadly heartworms but recently there also has been much concern over their involvement with West Nile virus. While we can avoid heartworm with the use of preventive medications, there are no such preventives for West Nile virus. The only method of prevention in endemic areas is active mosquito control. Fortunately, most dogs that have been exposed to the virus only developed flu-like symptoms and, to date, there have not been the large number of reported deaths in canines as seen in some other species.

MOSQUITO REPELLENT

Low concentrations of DEET (less than 10%), found in many human mosquito repellents, have been safely used in dogs but, in these concentrations, probably give only about two hours of protection. DEET may be safe in these small concentrations, but since it is not licensed for use on dogs, there is no research proving its safety for dogs. Products containing permethrin give the longest-lasting protection, perhaps two to four weeks. As DEET is not licensed for use on dogs, and both DEET and permethrin can be quite toxic to cats, appropriate care should be exercised. Other products, such as those containing oil of citronella, also have some mosquito-repellent activity, but typically have a relatively short duration of action.

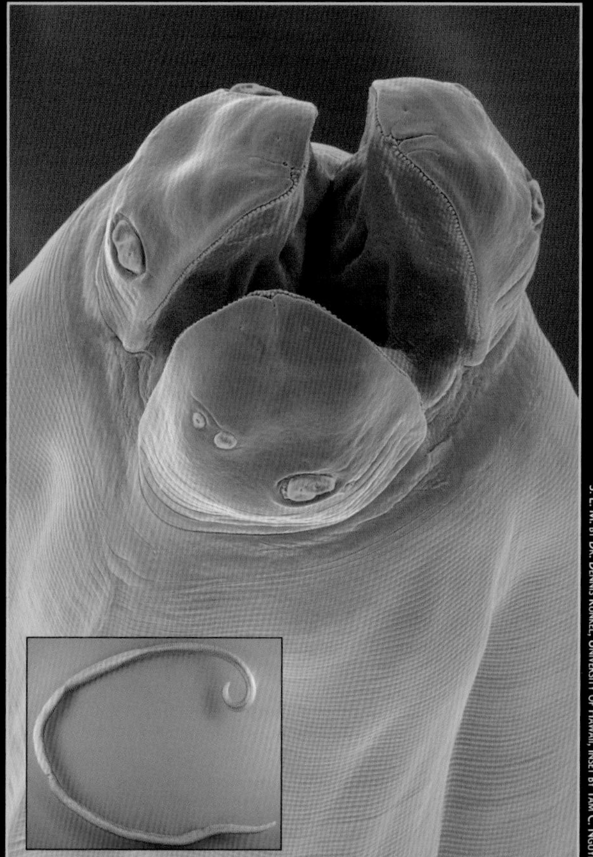

S. E. M. by Dr. Dennis Kunkel, University of Hawaii; Inset by Tam C. Nguyen.

ASCARID DANGERS

The most commonly encountered worms in dogs are roundworms known as ascarids. *Toxascaris leonine* and *Toxocara canis* are the two species that infect dogs. Subsisting in the dog's stomach and intestines, adult roundworms can grow to 7 inches in length and adult females can lay in excess of 200,000 eggs in a single day.

In humans, visceral larval migrans affects people who have ingested eggs of *Toxocara canis*, which frequently contaminates children's sandboxes, beaches and park grounds. The roundworms reside in the human's stomach and intestines, as they would in a dog's, but do not mature. Instead, they find their way to the liver, lungs and skin, or even to the heart or kidneys in severe cases. Deworming puppies is critical in preventing the infection in humans, and young children should never handle nursing pups who have not been dewormed.

The ascarid roundworm *Toxocara canis*, showing the mouth with three lips. INSET: Photomicrograph of the roundworm *Ascaris lumbricoides*.

INTERNAL PARASITES: WORMS

Ascarids

Ascarids are intestinal roundworms that rarely cause severe disease in dogs. Nonetheless, they are of major public health significance because they can be transferred to people. Sadly, it is children who are most commonly affected by the parasite, probably from inadvertently ingesting ascarid-contaminated soil. In fact, many yards and children's sandboxes contain appreciable numbers of ascarid eggs. So, while ascarids don't bite dogs or latch onto their intestines to suck blood, they do cause some nasty medical conditions in children and are best eradicated from our furry friends. Because pups can start passing ascarid eggs by three weeks of age, most parasite-control programs begin at two weeks of age and are repeated every two weeks until pups are eight weeks old. It is important to

HOOKED ON *ANCYLOSTOMA*

Adult dogs can become infected by the bloodsucking nematodes we commonly call hookworms via ingesting larvae from the ground or via the larvae penetrating the dog's skin. It is not uncommon for infected dogs to show no symptoms of hookworm infestation. Sometimes symptoms occur within ten days of exposure. These symptoms can include bloody diarrhea, anemia, loss of weight and general weakness. Dogs pass the hookworm eggs in their stools, which serves as the vet's method of identifying the infestation. The hookworm larvae can encyst themselves in the dog's tissues and be released when the dog is experiencing stress.

Caused by an *Ancylostoma* species whose common host is the dog, cutaneous larval migrans affects humans, causing itching and lumps and streaks beneath the surface of the skin.

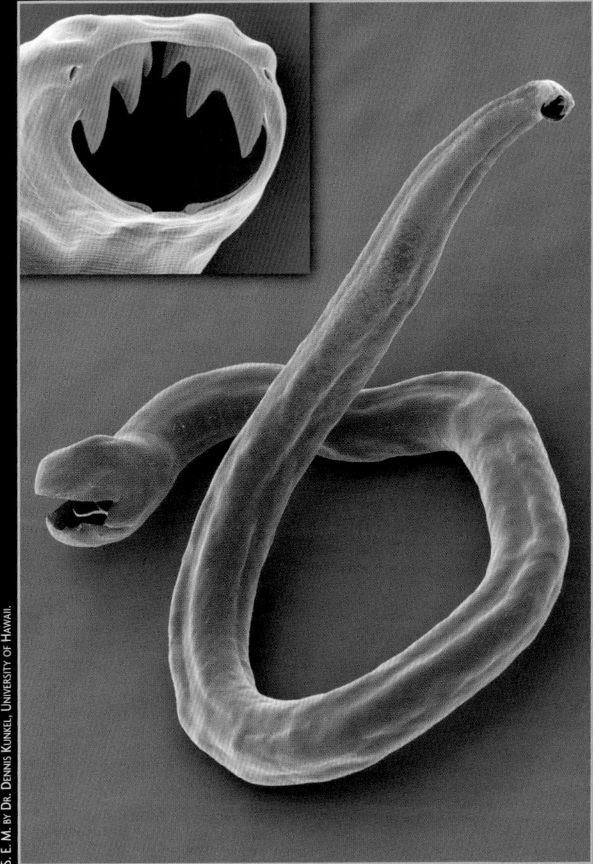

S. E. M. by Dr. Dennis Kunkel, University of Hawaii.

The hookworm *Ancylostoma caninum* infests the intestines of dogs. INSET: Note the row of hooks at the posterior end, used to anchor the worm to the intestinal wall.

realize that bitches can pass ascarids to their pups even if they test negative prior to whelping. Accordingly, bitches are best treated at the same time as the pups.

Hookworms

Unlike ascarids, hookworms do latch onto a dog's intestinal tract and can cause significant loss of blood and protein. Similar to ascarids, hookworms can be transmitted to humans, where they cause a condition known as cutaneous larval migrans. Dogs can become infected either by consuming the infective larvae or by the larvae's penetrating the skin directly. People most often get infected when they are lying on the ground (such as on a beach) and the larvae penetrate the skin. Yes, the larvae can penetrate through a beach blanket. Hookworms are typically susceptible to the same medications used to treat ascarids.

WHIPWORMS

Whipworms latch onto the lower aspects of the dog's colon and can cause cramping and diarrhea. Eggs do not start to appear in the dog's feces until about three months after the dog was infected. This worm has a peculiar life cycle, which makes it more difficult to control than ascarids or hookworms. The good thing is that whipworms rarely are transferred to people.

Some of the medications used to treat ascarids and hookworms are also effective against whipworms, but, in general, a separate treatment protocol is needed. Since most of the medications are effective against the adults but not the eggs or larvae, treatment is typically repeated in three weeks, and then often in three months as well. Unfortunately, since dogs don't develop resistance to whipworms, it is difficult to prevent them from getting reinfected if they visit soil contaminated with whipworm eggs.

WORM-CONTROL GUIDELINES

- Practice sanitary habits with your dog and home.
- Clean up after your dog and don't let him sniff or eat other dogs' droppings.
- Control insects and fleas in the dog's environment. Fleas, lice, cockroaches, beetles, mice and rats can act as hosts for various worms.
- Prevent dogs from eating uncooked meat, raw poultry and dead animals.
- Keep dogs and children from playing in sand and soil.
- Kennel dogs on cement or gravel; avoid dirt runs.
- Administer heartworm preventives regularly.
- Have your vet examine your dog's stools at your annual visits.
- Select a boarding kennel carefully so as to avoid contamination from other dogs or an unsanitary environment.
- Prevent dogs from roaming. Obey local leash laws.

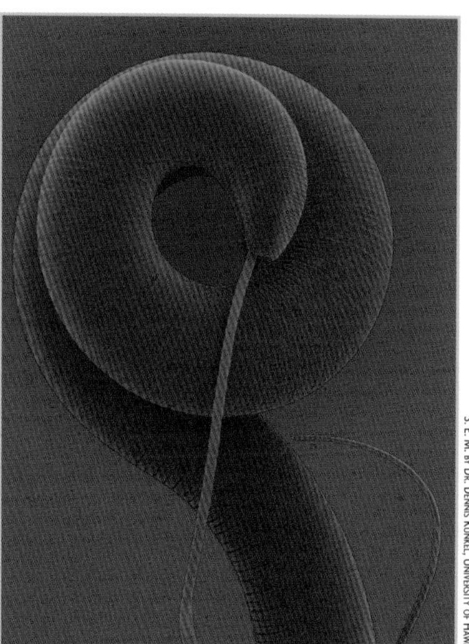

Adult whipworm, *Trichuris* sp., an intestinal parasite.

S.E.M. BY DR. DENNIS KUNKEL, UNIVERSITY OF HAWAII.

TAPEWORMS

There are many different species of tapeworm that affect dogs, but *Dipylidium caninum* is probably the most common and is spread by fleas. Flea larvae feed on organic debris and tapeworm eggs in the environment and, when a dog chews at himself and manages to ingest fleas, he might get a dose of tapeworm at the same time. The tapeworm then develops further in the intestine of the dog.

The tapeworm itself, which is a parasitic flatworm that latches onto the intestinal wall, is composed of numerous segments. When the segments break off into the intestine (as proglottids), they may accumulate around the rectum, like grains of rice. While this tapeworm is disgusting in its behavior, it is not directly communicable to humans (although humans can also get infected by swallowing fleas).

S. E. M. by Dr. Dennis Kunkel, University of Hawaii.

A dog tapeworm proglottid (body segment).

A much more dangerous flatworm is *Echinococcus multilocularis*, which is typically found in foxes, coyotes and wolves. The eggs are passed in the feces and infect rodents, and, when dogs eat the rodents, the dogs can be infected by thousands of adult tapeworms. While the parasites don't cause many problems in dogs, this is considered the most lethal worm infection that people can get. Take appropriate precautions if you live in an area in which these tapeworms are found. Do not use mulch that may contain feces of dogs, cats or wildlife, and discourage your pets from hunting wildlife. Treat these tapeworm infections aggressively in pets, because if humans get infected, approximately half die.

Heartworms

Heartworm disease is caused by the parasite *Dirofilaria immitis* and is seen in dogs around the world. A member of the roundworm group, it is spread between dogs by the bite of an infected mosquito. The mosquito injects infective larvae into the dog's skin with its bite, and these larvae develop under the skin for a period of time before making their way to the heart. There they develop into adults, which grow and create blockages of the heart, lungs and major blood vessels there. They also start producing offspring (microfilariae)

S. E. M. by Dr. Dennis Kunkel, University of Hawaii.

The dog tapeworm *Taenia pisiformis*.

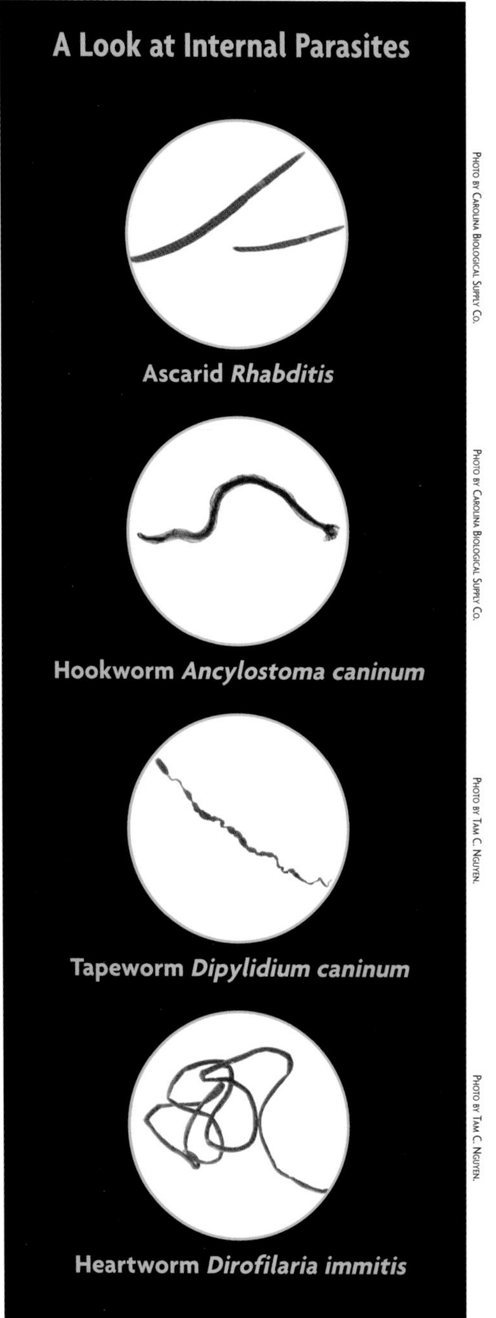

A Look at Internal Parasites

Ascarid *Rhabditis*

PHOTO BY CAROLINA BIOLOGICAL SUPPLY CO.

Hookworm *Ancylostoma caninum*

PHOTO BY CAROLINA BIOLOGICAL SUPPLY CO.

Tapeworm *Dipylidium caninum*

PHOTO BY TAM C. NGUYEN.

Heartworm *Dirofilaria immitis*

PHOTO BY TAM C. NGUYEN.

and these microfilariae circulate in the bloodstream, waiting to hitch a ride when the next mosquito bites. Once in the mosquito, the microfilariae develop into infective larvae and the entire process is repeated.

When dogs get infected with heartworm, over time they tend to develop symptoms associated with heart disease, such as coughing, exercise intolerance and potentially many other manifestations. Diagnosis is confirmed by either seeing the microfilariae themselves in blood samples or using immunologic tests (antigen testing) to identify the presence of adult heartworms. Since antigen tests measure the presence of adult heartworms and microfilarial tests measure offspring produced by adults, neither are positive until six to seven months after the initial infection. However, the beginning of damage can occur by fifth-stage larvae as early as three months after infection. Thus it is possible for dogs to be harboring problem-causing larvae for up to three months before either type of test would identify an infection.

The good news is that there are great protocols available for preventing heartworm in dogs. Testing is critical in the process, and it is important to understand the benefits as well as the limitations of such testing. All dogs six months of age or older that have not been on continuous heartworm-preventive medication should be

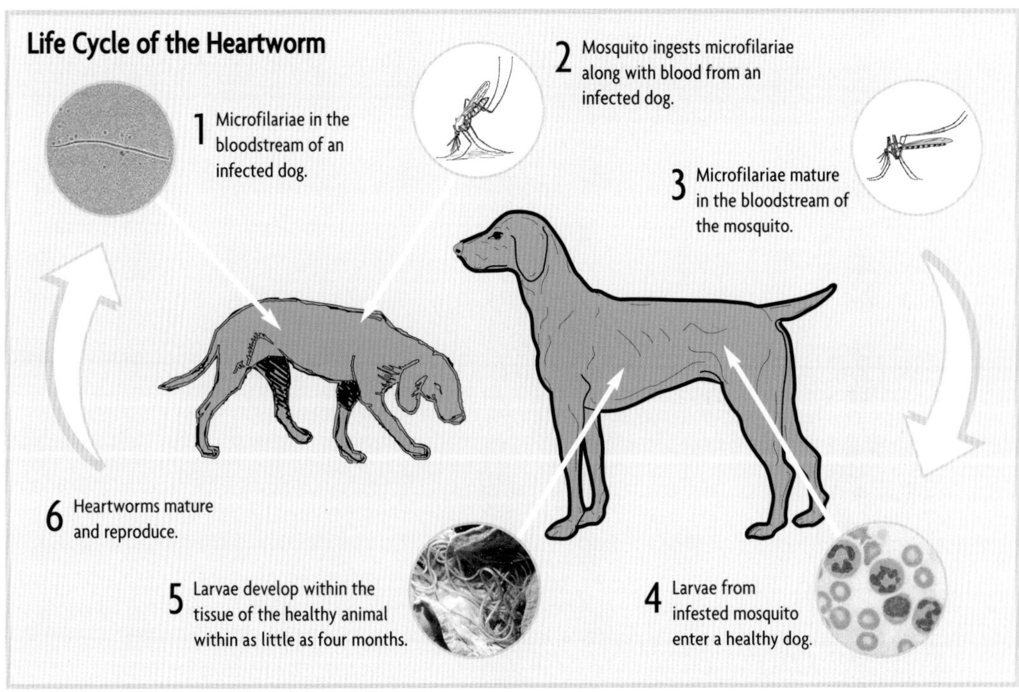

screened with microfilarial or antigen tests. For dogs receiving preventive medication, periodic antigen testing helps assess the effectiveness of the preventives. The American Heartworm Society guidelines suggest that annual retesting may not be necessary when owners have absolutely provided continuous heartworm prevention. Retesting on a two- to three-year interval may be sufficient in these cases. However, your veterinarian will likely have specific guidelines under which heartworm preventives will be prescribed, and many prefer to err on the side of safety and retest annually.

It is indeed fortunate that heartworm is relatively easy to prevent, because treatments can be as life-threatening as the disease itself. Treatment requires a two-step process that kills the adult heartworms first and then the microfilariae. Prevention is obviously preferable; this involves a once-monthly oral or topical treatment. The most common oral preventives include ivermectin (not suitable for some breeds), moxidectin and milbemycin oxime; the once-a-month topical drug selamectin provides heartworm protection in addition to flea, some types of tick and other parasite controls.

SHOWING YOUR NORWEGIAN ELKHOUND

Is dog showing in your blood? Are you excited by the idea of gaiting your handsome Norwegian Elkhound around the ring to the thunderous applause of an enthusiastic audience? Are you certain that your beloved Norwegian Elkhound is flawless? You are not alone! Every loving owner thinks that his dog has no faults, or too few to mention. No matter how many times an owner reads the breed standard, he cannot find any faults in his aristocratic companion dog. If this sounds like you, and if you are considering entering your Norwegian Elkhound in a dog show, here are some basic questions to ask yourself:

- Did you purchase a "show-quality" puppy from the breeder?
- Is your puppy at least six months of age?
- Does the puppy exhibit correct show type for his breed?
- Does your puppy have any disqualifying faults?
- Is your Norwegian Elkhound registered with the American Kennel Club?
- How much time do you have to devote to training, grooming, conditioning and exhibiting your dog?
- Do you understand the rules and regulations of a dog show?
- Do you have time to learn how to show your dog properly?
- Do you have the financial resources to invest in showing your dog?
- Will you show the dog yourself or hire a professional handler?
- Do you have a vehicle that can accommodate your weekend trips to the dog shows?

Success in the show ring requires more than a pretty face, a waggy tail and a pocketful of liver. Even though dog shows can be exciting and enjoyable, the sport of conformation makes great demands on the exhibitors and the dogs. Winning exhibitors live for their dogs, devoting time and money to their dogs' presentation, conditioning and training. Very

AKC GROUPS

For showing purposes, the American Kennel Club divides its recognized breeds into seven groups: Hounds, Sporting Dogs, Working Dogs, Terriers, Toys, Non-Sporting Dogs and Herding Dogs.

few novices, even those with good dogs, will find themselves in the winners' circle, though it does happen. Don't be disheartened, though. Every exhibitor began as a novice and worked his way up to the Group ring. It's the "working your way up" part that you must keep in mind.

Assuming that you have purchased a puppy of the correct type and quality for showing, let's begin to examine the world of showing and what's required to get started. Although the entry fee into a dog show is nominal, there are lots of other hidden costs involved with "finishing" your Norwegian Elkhound, that is, making him a champion. Things like equipment, travel, training and conditioning all cost money. A more serious campaign will include fees for a professional handler, boarding, cross-country travel and advertising. Top-winning show dogs can represent a very considerable investment—over $100,000 has been spent in campaigning some dogs. (The investment can be less, of course, for owners who don't use professional handlers.)

Many owners, on the other hand, enter their "average" Norwegian Elkhounds in dog shows for the fun and enjoyment of it. Dog showing makes an absorbing hobby, with many rewards for dogs and owners alike. If you're having fun, meeting other people who share your interests and enjoying the overall experience, you likely will catch the "bug." Once the dog-show bug bites, its effects can last a lifetime; it's certainly much better than a deer tick! Soon you will be envisioning yourself in the center ring at the Westminster Kennel Club Dog Show in New York City, competing for the prestigious Best in Show cup. This magical dog show is televised annually from Madison Square Garden, and the victorious dog becomes a celebrity overnight.

Here's Pat Trotter with Ch. Vin-Melca's Marketta in the Best in Show ring at Westminster Kennel Club in 1995. Marketta is the only Quaker Oats Award winner whose parents were both Quaker Oats Award winners too.

AKC CONFORMATION BASICS

Visiting a dog show as a spectator is a great place to begin your journey into the world of dog showing. Pick up the show catalog to find out what time your breed is being shown, who is judging the breed and in which ring the classes will be held. To start, Norwegian Elkhounds compete

Ch. Vin-Melca's Bombardier, the sire of Marketta, won 39 Bests in Show and was a Quaker Oats Award winner.

against other Norwegian Elkhounds, and the winner is selected as Best of Breed by the judge. This is the procedure for each breed. At a group show, all of the Best of Breed winners go on to compete for Group One in their respective groups. For example, all Best of Breed winners in a given group compete against each other; this is done for all seven groups. Finally, all seven group winners go head to head in the ring for the Best in Show award.

What most spectators don't understand is the basic idea of conformation. A dog show is often referred as a "conformation" show. This means that the judge should decide how each dog stacks up (conforms) to the breed standard for his given breed: how well does this Norwegian Elkhound conform to the ideal representative detailed in the standard? Ideally, this is what happens. In reality, however, this ideal often gets slighted as the judge compares Norwegian Elkhound #1 to Norwegian Elkhound #2. Again, the ideal is that each dog is judged based on his merits in comparison to his breed standard, not in comparison to the other dogs in the ring. It is easier for judges to compare dogs of the same breed to decide which they think is the better specimen; in the Group and Best in Show ring, however, it is very difficult to compare one breed to another, like apples to oranges. Thus the dog's conformation to the breed standard—not to mention advertising dollars and good handling—is essential to success in conformation shows. The dog described in the standard (the standard for each AKC breed is written and

BECOMING A CHAMPION

An official AKC championship of record requires that a dog accumulate 15 points under three different judges, including two "majors" under different judges. Points are awarded based on the number of dogs entered into competition, varying from breed to breed and place to place. A win of three, four or five points is considered a "major." The AKC annually assigns a schedule of points to adjust for variations that accompany a breed's popularity and the population of a given area.

approved by the breed's national parent club and then submitted to the AKC for approval) is the perfect dog of that breed, and breeders keep their eye on the standard when they choose which dogs to breed, hoping to get closer and closer to that elusive ideal with each litter.

Another good first step for the novice is to join a dog club. You will be astonished by the many and different kinds of dog clubs in the country, with about 5,000 clubs holding events every year. Most clubs require that prospective new members present two letters of recommendation from existing members. Perhaps you've made some friends visiting a show held by a particular club and you would like to join that club. Dog clubs may specialize in a single breed, like a local or regional Norwegian Elkhound club, or in a specific pursuit, such as obedience, tracking or hunting tests. There are all-breed clubs for all dog enthusiasts; they sponsor special training days, seminars on topics like grooming or handling or lectures on breeding or canine genetics. There are also clubs that specialize in certain types of dogs, like hounds, hunting dogs, companion dogs, etc.

A parent club is the national organization, sanctioned by the AKC, which promotes and safeguards its breed in the country. The Norwegian Elkhound Association of America was formed around 1930 and can be contacted on the Internet at www.neaa.net. The parent club holds an annual national specialty show, usually in a different city each year, in which many of the country's top dogs, handlers and breeders gather to compete. At a specialty show, only members of a single breed are invited to participate. There are also group specialties, in which all members of a group are invited. For more information about dog clubs in your area, contact the AKC at www.akc.org on the Internet or

FIVE CLASSES AT SHOWS

At most AKC all-breed shows, there are five regular classes offered: Puppy, Novice, Bred-by-Exhibitor, American-bred and Open. The Puppy Class is usually divided as 6 to 9 months of age and 9 to 12 months of age. When deciding in which class to enter your dog, whether male or female, you must carefully check the show schedule to make sure that you have selected the right class. Depending on the age of the dog, previous first-place wins and the sex of the dog, you must make the best choice. It is possible to enter a one-year-old dog who has not won sufficient first places in any of the non-Puppy Classes, though the competition is more intense the further you progress from the Puppy Class.

Some Elkhounds just can't contain their excitement over being in the show ring!

write them at their Raleigh, NC address.

OTHER TYPES OF COMPETITION

In addition to conformation shows, the AKC holds a variety of other competitive events. Obedience trials, agility trials and tracking trials are open to all breeds, while hunting tests, field trials, lure coursing, herding tests and trials, earthdog tests and coonhound events are limited to specific breeds or groups of breeds. The Junior Showmanship program is offered to aspiring young handlers and their dogs, and the Canine Good Citizen® Program is an all-around good-behavior test open to all dogs, pure-bred and mixed.

Obedience Trials

By Kari Olson

In the US, obedience trials have grown more and more popular, and now more than 2,000 trials each year attract over 100,000 dogs and their owners. Any dog registered with the AKC, regardless of neutering or other disqualifications that would preclude entry in conformation competition, can participate in obedience trials.

There are three levels of difficulty in obedience competition. The first (and easiest) level is the Novice, in which dogs can earn the Companion Dog (CD) title. The intermediate level is the Open level, in which the Companion Dog Excellent (CDX) title is awarded. The advanced level is the Utility level, in which dogs compete for the Utility Dog (UD) title. Classes at each level are further divided into "A" and "B," with "A" for beginners and "B" for those with more experience. In order to win a title at a given level, a dog must earn three "legs." A "leg" is accomplished when a dog scores 170 or higher (200 is a perfect score). The scoring system gets a little trickier when you understand that a dog must score more than 50% of the points available for each exercise in order to actually earn the points. Available points for each exercise range between 20 and 40.

A dog must complete different exercises at each level of obedi-

The Norwegian Elkhound's gait should appear agile and effortless, indicative of a sturdy build and capacity for work.

ence. The Novice exercises are the easiest, with the Open and finally the Utility levels progressing in difficulty. Examples of Novice exercises are on- and off-lead heeling, a figure-8 pattern, performing a recall (or come), long sit and long down and standing for examination. In the Open level, the Novice-level exercises are required again, but this time without a leash and for longer durations. In addition, the dog must clear a broad jump, retrieve over a jump and drop on recall. In the Utility level, the exercises are quite difficult, including executing basic commands based on hand signals, following a complex heeling pattern, locating articles based on scent discrimination and completing jumps at the handler's direction.

Once he's earned the UD title, a dog can go on to win the prestigious title of Utility Dog Excellent (UDX) by winning "legs" in ten shows. The first conformation champion to earn the UDT title (UD plus Tracking title) was Ch. Crafdal Thor Mhors Paulette UDT. Additionally, Utility Dogs who win "legs" in Open B and Utility B earn points toward the lofty title of Obedience Trial Champion (OTCh.). Established in 1977 by the

CANINE GOOD CITIZEN® PROGRAM

Have you ever considered getting your dog "certified"? The AKC's Canine Good Citizen® Program affords your dog just that opportunity. Your dog shows that he is a well-behaved canine citizen, using the basic training and good manners you have taught him, by taking a series of ten tests that illustrate that he can behave properly at home, in a public place and around other dogs. The tests are administered by participating dog clubs, colleges, 4-H clubs, Scouts and other community groups and are open to all pure-bred and mixed-breed dogs. Upon passing the ten tests, the suffix CGC is then applied to your dog's name.

The ten tests are: 1. Accepting a friendly stranger; 2. Sitting politely for petting; 3. Appearance and grooming; 4. Walking on a lead; 5. Walking through a group of people; 6. Sit, down and stay on command; 7. Coming when called; 8. Meeting another dog; 9. Calm reaction to distractions; 10. Separation from owner.

FOR MORE INFORMATION...

For reliable up-to-date information about registration, dog shows and other canine competitions, contact one of the national registries by mail or via the Internet.

American Kennel Club
5580 Centerview Dr., Raleigh, NC 27606-3390
www.akc.org

United Kennel Club
100 E. Kilgore Road, Kalamazoo, MI 49002
www.ukcdogs.com

Canadian Kennel Club
89 Skyway Ave., Suite 100, Etobicoke, Ontario
M9W 6R4 Canada
www.ckc.ca

AKC, this title requires a dog to earn 100 points as well as three first places in a combination of Open B and Utility B classes under three different judges.

Norwegian Elkhounds have long participated in obedience, and today in this age of positive reinforcement, they are achieving more success than ever. Elkhounds still need to know when they are wrong, but trying to force an Elkhound to do your bidding rarely works. This breed is very intelligent, but is also sensitive and the dogs can be independent thinkers; this is what used to be called stubborn!

The first two AKC Obedience Trial Champions were both owned, handled and trained by Don Rotier, who seemed to have the inside information on just how to get this breed to conform to his wishes. The two Elkhounds were Am./Can. OTCh. Camalot's Bella Tigra (imported as a puppy from Norway and co-owned by Mari Misbeek) and Am./Can. OTCh. Camalot's Trulle Ayla UD (owned by Marilyn Rotier and trained and handled by Don). Tigra's time was before the age of computers so she has been omitted from the AKC records for Lifetime OTCh. points, but will always remain in the breed's annals as the first OTCh. Elkhound. Ayla is listed as second in accumulated OTCh. points, numbering 187.

Following these two came only two more OTCh. Elkhounds. Ch./OTCh. Camalot's Priti Babe UDX8, bred by Mari Misbeek and owned by Ann M. Nowakowski, was not only the first conformation and obedience champion but she amassed the highest number of OTCh. points (numbering 310 and going strong). She was also the very first Norwegian Elkhound to earn a UDX title. In 2005 the AKC began a numbering system to show how many times the dog has earned the title; she's done it eight times so far.

The fourth AKC OTCh. Norwegian Elkhound was a rescue dog, a hound so wild that her previous owners were on the verge of putting her to sleep. However her situation was discovered by a well-known trainer who obtained

VERSATILE COMPANION AWARDS

The AKC awards Versatile Companion Dog (VCD) and Versatile Companion Champion (VCCh.) titles to dogs that excel in multiple areas of competition—obedience, agility and tracking. There are four levels of the VCD: VCD1 for earning the CD, NA, NAJ, TD or CD, NAP, NJP, TD; VCD2 for earning CDX, OA, OAJ, TD or CDX, OAP, OJP, TD; VCD3 for earning UD, AX, AXJ, TDX or UD, AXP, AJP, TDX; and VCD4 for earning UDX, MX, MXJ, VST or UDX, MXP, MJP, VST. The VCCh. title is awarded to dogs who have earned the OTCh., MACH and CT.

The first four Norwegian Elkhounds to receive Versatility titles were a dam, her two sons and a rescue dog. UACHX, U-UD, Can. OTCh./Ch. Vikro's Bright Flame UDT, VCD2, AX, AXJ, HIC, TDI, TT, OVNEX was bred by Vikiro Norwegian Elkhounds and owned by Kari Olson. Her two sons are Berserker and Brottsjo. "Brenne" has three other offspring from this amazing litter: one male titled in obedience and agility and two females that both became service dogs to their owners. Brenne herself earned four UD titles, three UDX legs, three High in Trial awards and three High Combined awards. She also was an Agility Champion. Her tracking title was the most exciting, and she loved tracking even more than obedience. The fourth VCD dog is a level 1 named Jessie Lizbeth Green CD, TDX, NA, NAJ, VCD1, owned by Sue Ellen Green.

Ch. Vikro's Bright Flame, known at home and in the ring as Brenne, is the dam of many of top performance dogs, including Berserker and Brottsjo. Owner, Kari Olson.

the dog for one of her students looking for a challenge. Mindy Costanza, the new owner and handler, harnessed her drive and energy by working obedience with her. This rescue Elkhound became OTCh. Cosmit's Brenne Lyn Strale UDX4, MX, AXJ, a top obedience and agility dog.

There are notable dogs who performed very well but with the fierce OTCh. competition in the AKC did not win a first or second enough times to earn the 100 points needed. Many times the score was so close it was heartbreaking, as time after time they missed the needed placement by just a point. After all, these are creative dogs and they seem sometimes to have a sense of humor (with the joke on the handler). The highest scoring of these dogs are Ch. Ravenswood Cloudberry UDX3, owned by

Susan M. Goss, 89 points; Harley's Shady Lady UD, owned by Terry Ruberto McCullogh, 45 points; UCD Ch. Liseldun Solv Sternje Vinsja UDX, owned by Steven and Renee Schmidt, 32 points; and Nakita UDX4, owned by John and Verna Tarnowsky, 32 points.

Among these high scorers is Visnja, bred by Barbara Roby, who won High in Trial at the national specialty as well as Best of Opposite Sex. He participated in three AKC Invitational Competitions. His lineage also goes back to that smart Camalot line of dogs that came down from Mari Misbeek's Norwegian imports. He was a fabulous heeler, with attention and accuracy and wonderful wins, but his greatest contribution was in passing on his willingness to work. No matter what they attempt, his puppies try their best to please their owners. This is not the attitude of all Elkhounds. The outcome of the breedings were especially successful in bitches of the Peer Gynt, Longships and Wil-Mar kennels. Vinsja has many titled offspring in conformation, obedience, agility and tracking. In recent years, he has had two Peer Gynt, three Wil-Mar and three Longships offspring competing in obedience and agility at the same time. His daughter, Ch. Peer Gynt Reyk Javik at Rijeka OA, OAJ, bred by Marlene Oliver and owner-trainer Renee Schmidt, is a top obedience dog who also has a conformation career.

Ch. Liseldun Solv Sternje Vinsja UDX, owned by Steven and Renee Schmidt, among the top-scoring Elkhounds on the obedience scene.

Vinsja's son Ch./MACH Longships Sealine Berserker VCD2, UDX, AXP, NJP, bred by Kari Olson and owned by Larry and Cindy Lovig, earned his UDX by age two. Next he became a Master Agility Champion, won four Top Agility Dog awards and won a Top Versatility Dog award from the NEAA. He is continuing to show in obedience at specialties, run Preferred Agility and train for the TDX test.

His littermate has been awarded the national club's honor of Top Obedience Dog twice as well as Top Versatility Dog. He is UACHX, UOCH, Can. OTCh. AKC/UKC Ch. Longships Icebreaker UDX2, TD, ASCA/SKC

UD, MX, AXP, MXJ, OJP, NCP, HIC, TDI ,VCD2, OVNEX, owned by breeder Kari Olson. "Brottsjo" has 22 OTCh. points and has placed in the group at obedience invitationals. He has the distinction of being the only United Kennel Club (UKC) Triple Champion (conformation, agility and obedience). He also is a Canadian OTCh. and holds five different Utility Dog titles. He could be called the specialty "specialist" as he has won over 23 specialty High in Trial awards and 11 High Combined wins. He recently retired from regular obedience due to an injury and is now showing in Rally Obedience at the Excellent level.

Agility Trials
by Kari Olson

Agility trials became sanctioned by the AKC in August 1994, when the first licensed agility trials were held. Since that time, agility certainly has grown in popularity by leaps and bounds, literally! The AKC allows all registered breeds (including Miscellaneous Class breeds) to participate, providing the dog is 12 months of age or older. Agility is designed so that the handler demonstrates how well the dog can work at his side. The handler directs his dog through, over, under and around an obstacle course that includes jumps, tires, the dog walk, weave poles, pipe tunnels, collapsed tunnels and more. While working his way through the course, the dog must keep one eye and ear on the handler and the rest of his body on the course. The handler runs along with the dog, giving verbal and hand signals to guide the dog through the course.

Ch./MACH Longships Sealine Berserker, VCD2, UDX, AXP, NJP, bred by Kari Olson and owned by Larry and Cindy Lovig, one of the few Elkhounds to earn a Versatility award.

The structure, energy and speed of the Norwegian Elkhound create a dog able to make the leaps, quick turns and running spurts that easily give a dog an edge in this sport. These are the same qualities that give Elkhounds success in hunting in their native country. However, they are very independent and intelligent, and often go through a phase during learning of wanting to run their own course. The key is to have patience, persistence, a positive attitude and often use food as incentive. The dogs will eventually become a team with their owners and come to love agility simply for the joy of jumping and being able to do things with their owners.

Brottsjo is short for Kari Olson's multi-titled, multi-talented Elkhound whose registered name is Ch. Longships Icebreaker. He has the distinction of being the UKC's only Triple Champion Elkhound.

This is not a breed that blindly obeys his owner, it is more like a real partnership between man and dog. It is quite a thrill to see a beautiful perfect run of an Elkhound and handler.

The first organization to promote agility trials in the US was the United States Dog Agility Association, Inc. (USDAA). Established in 1986, the USDAA sparked the formation of many member clubs around the country. To participate in USDAA trials, dogs must be at least 18 months of age.

The USDAA and AKC both offer titles to winning dogs, although the exercises and requirements of the two organizations differ. Agility Dog (AD), Advanced Agility Dog (AAD) and Master Agility Dog (MAD) are the titles offered by the USDAA, while the AKC offers Novice Agility (NA), Open Agility (OA), Agility Excellent (AX) and Master Agility Excellent (MX). Beyond these four AKC titles, dogs can win additional titles in "jumper" classes: Jumper with Weave Novice (NAJ), Open (OAJ) and Excellent (MXJ). The ultimate title in AKC agility is MACH, Master Agility Champion. Dogs can continue to add number designations to the MACH title, indicating how many times the dog has met the title's requirements (MACH1, MACH2 and so on).

Agility trials are a great way to keep your dog active, and they will keep you running, too! You should join a local agility club to learn more about the sport. These clubs offer sessions in which you can introduce your dog to the various obstacles as well as training classes to prepare him for competition. In no time, your dog will be climbing A-frames, crossing the dog walk

The Norwegian Elkhound excels in agility trials, as evidenced by this weaving wonder.

and flying over hurdles, all with you right beside him. Your heart will leap every time your dog jumps through the hoop—and you'll be having just as much (if not more) fun!

Recently the number of Elkhounds in AKC agility has grown slowly from a handful of dogs to dozens. Most Elkhounds that compete in agility today also have training in obedience and even tracking. It is an advantage to cross-train as some obedience is needed in agility to succeed. Many of the Elkhounds competing in agility are breed champions also.

Norwegian Elkhounds started participating in agility in the late 1980s. Winning Top Dog in Agility Match in November 1989 was U-CDX Olson's Bjorna av Bondegard CDX, Can. CD, TDI, owned by Kari Olson. She went on to receive what is believed to be the first qualifying score in any United States Agility titling event. She was awarded a Certificate of Merit in 1990, to indicate she had a qualifying score in one of the first trials sponsored by the National Committee for Dog Agility (NCDA), currently in the United Kennel Club program. She was already 11 years old at that time! In addition to AKC and USDAA trials, Elkhounds also can participate in UKC and North American Dog Agility Council (NADAC) trials.

In 1994, the first year of AKC agility-titling classes, V-NATCH, UATCH Ch. Midnight Sun's Grin N Berrit MX, AXJ, CDX, AAD, SM, GS-E, RS-E, VNEX made Elkhound history by becoming the top AKC agility dog all-breeds! She was bred by Sandy Groleau and co-owner Barbara Budny, and handled by co-owner Richard Budny. Berrit also was the Top Hound in the first AKC national competition and was the first of the breed to earn both the NCDA (UKC) Agility Championship title and the AKC Master Agility title. She competed also in USDAA and NADAC at the elite levels, becoming the first Elkhound to earn the USDAA Veterans Agility Championship (V-NATCH). In her career in all 4 agility venues, she amassed well over 300 first places during her career.

Ch. Midnight Sun's Grin N Berrit broke all the records when she became the first Norwegian Elkhound to be top agility dog all-breeds. She is owned by Richard and Barbara Budny.

The year 2003 marked a triumph for the Elkhound, as MACH Ch. Longships Sealine Berserker VCD2, TD, OAP, NAJ, OVNEX became the breed's first

Ch. Wil-Mar's Hot 'N' Spicey Nike, owned by Rhonda Levinowsky and Linda Syner, has titled in agility even as a senior.

(and so far only) Master Agility. Bred by Kari Olson and owned by Larry and Cindy Lovig, Berserker was superbly handled by Larry for many years on the course (and over many jumps) to the MACH. He was also the Norwegian Elkhound Association of America's top agility contender for four years. After earning his MACH, this wonderful dog participated at the Preferred level (lower jumps and slower times) handled by the Lovigs' six-year-old son Thorson. The team of Thorson and Berserker has been so heartwarming to watch. One example was when the dog exited a tunnel and waited for the little boy to catch up with him!

Luckily most Norwegian Elkhounds live a healthy, long productive life. Although hip dysplasia can be a problem in the breed, it is often mild enough that a well-muscled dog can still jump, even compete for many years. The Preferred agility classes, open to dogs of any age, are wonderful for older dogs or their owners who would like a little lower jump height and more time.

A few outstanding seniors excelled in the Preferred classes. Ch. Wil-Mar's Hot 'N' Spicey Nike CDX, AX, OAP, AXJ, OAJ, AAD, bred by Marlene and William Schlichtig and owned by Rhonda Levinowsky and Linda Syner, retired at age 14, upon the vet's advice. Nike was another of our forerunners, competing in agility most of her life in all venues, and achieving great success in USDAA trials. She is one of a number of Wil-Mar dogs that have excelled in agility and performance areas of competition. Another senior, 12-year-old Ch. Peer Gynt's Top of the Eighth UD, AX, MXP2, AXJ, MJP2, bred by Marlene Oliver and owned by the breeder and Tom and Carol Slattery, was the first Elkhound and hound to achieve most of the AKC Preferred titles. "Rookie," under Tom's capable handling, proved to become more and more reliable and virtually whizzed through his performance titles, becoming the only Elkhound thus far to achieve the MXP2 or MXJ2 titles (the equivalent of qualifying 20 times in each class).

Another big winner, Multi SBIS, UACHX, U-CDX, AKC/UKC Ch. Norelka's City Slicker CDX, RN, MX, NAP, MXJ, NJP, MAD, CGC, JM, EAC, EJC-V, RV-E, JV-E, GV-O, SAD, TDI, HIC, VNEX, owned by Tracy Smith, is the first Norwegian Elkhound to earn a MAD. "Impi," as he is fondly called, is still competing in obedience and Preferred agility trials.

Some owners find the challenge of a Norwegian Elkhound in agility to be too frustrating and turn to more traditional breeds. But for those who admire this breed's grace and spirit, there is nothing more satisfying than seeing your beautiful Elkhound complete a clean run and earn a new title.

Ch. Peer Gynt Top of the Eighth, owned by Marlene Oliver and Tom and Carol Slattery, is the first Elkhound to earn most of the Preferred agility titles.

Rally Obedience

In 2005 the AKC began a new program called Rally Obedience. This is a less formal activity yet titles are awarded. There are four levels of competition: Novice, Advanced, Excellent and Advanced/Excellent. The dog and handler do a series of exercises designed by the judge and are timed. The handlers are encouraged to talk to their dog as they work through the course. The dogs love this and it shows by their animation and energy.

Within just a few weeks of Rally's inception, the first Rally-titled Norwegian Elkhound emerged: U-CD Wrathwoods Lasting UD, RN, NA, NAJ, NJC, bred by Lynda Tarnowski and owned by Dona Barsul. "Merlin" has also been trained in search and rescue.

The first Elkhound to earn an advanced title was Brottsjo, whose "Versatility" is well known. Many of the dogs who participate in one sport also do so in the others. While most of the first Rally titles earned by Elkhounds have gone to seasoned obedience dogs, it's encouraging that some newcomers have also earned awards. Rally is a

Ch. Snojagers Step Up to the Bat MX, MJX, proving how patient and obedient the Elkhound can be!

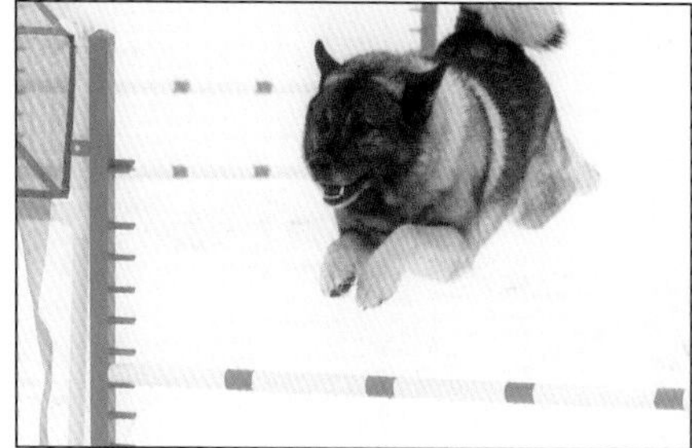
Ch. Norelka's City Slicker, owned by Tracy Smith, goes by the call name "Impi."

good way for a beginner to start out in obedience, and we hope that it will become a stepping stone to the obedience world and we will see many more Elkhounds and owners coming into the ring.

TRACKING

Tracking tests are exciting ways to test your Norwegian Elkhound's instinctive scenting ability on a competitive level. All dogs have a nose, and all breeds are welcome in tracking tests. The first AKC-licensed tracking test took place in 1937 as part of the Utility level at an obedience trial, and thus competitive tracking was officially begun. The first title, Tracking Dog (TD), was offered in 1947, ten years after the first official tracking test. It was not until 1980 that the AKC added the title Tracking Dog Excellent (TDX), which was followed by the title Versatile Surface Tracking (VST) in 1995. Champion Tracker (CT) is awarded to a dog who has earned all three of those titles.

Here's the very versatile Brottsjo, the first dog to earn an advanced Rally title.

The TD level is the first and most basic level in tracking, progressing in difficulty to the TDX and then the VST. A dog must follow a track laid by a human 30 to 120 minutes prior in order to earn the TD title. The track is about 500 yards long and contains up to 5 directional changes. At the next level, the TDX, the dog must follow a 3- to 5-hour-old track over a course that is up to 1,000 yards long and has up to 7 directional changes. In the most difficult level, the VST, the track is up to 5 hours old and located in an urban setting.

The first Norwegian Elkhound believed to be titled in conformation, obedience and tracking was Ch. Leif of Dragondell CDX, TD, having earned his tracking title in 1961, owned by former Hon. Judge William Timbers. The first conformation champion Utility Tracker was Ch. Crafdal Thor Mhors Paulette UDT, owned by Paul and Nina Ross, having earned her TD in 1978.

BEHAVIOR OF YOUR NORWEGIAN ELKHOUND

You chose your dog because something clicked the minute you set eyes on him. Or perhaps it seemed that the dog selected you and that's what clinched the deal. Either way, you are now investing time and money in this dog, a true pal and an outstanding member of the family. Everything about him is perfect—well, almost perfect. Remember, he is a dog! For that matter, how does he think *you're* doing?

A bright dog with an independent streak, the Elkhound can require some convincing to see things his owner's way.

AGGRESSION

While the Norwegian Elkhound is generally not an aggressive breed, aggression is a problem that concerns all responsible dog owners. "Aggression" is a word that is often misunderstood and is sometimes even used to describe what is actually normal canine behavior. For example, it's normal for puppies to growl when playing tug-of-war. It's puppy talk. There are different forms of dog aggression, but all are degrees of dominance, indicating that the dog, not his master, is (or thinks he is) in control. When the dog feels that he (or his control of the situation) is threatened, he will respond. The extent of the aggressive behavior varies with individual dogs. It is not at all pleasant to see bared teeth or to hear your dog growl or snarl, but these are

> **PROFESSIONAL HELP**
>
> Every trainer and behaviorist asks, "Why didn't you come to me sooner?" Pet owners often don't want to admit that anything is wrong with their dogs. A dog's problem often is due to the dog and his owner mixing their messages, which will only get worse. Don't put it off; consult a professional to find out whether or not the problem is serious enough to require professional intervention.

signs of behavior that, if left uncorrected, can become extremely dangerous. A word of warning here: never challenge an aggressive dog. He is unpredictable and therefore unreliable to approach.

Nothing gets a "hello" from strangers on the street quicker than walking a puppy, but people should ask permission before petting your dog so you can tell him to sit in order to receive the admiring pats. If a hand comes down over the dog's head and he shrinks back, ask the person to bring his hand up, underneath the pup's chin. Now you're correcting strangers, too! But if you don't, it could make your dog afraid of strangers, which in turn can lead to fear-biting. Socialization prevents much aggression before it rears its ugly head.

Practicing basic obedience is a simple way to continually reinforce your role as leader.

DOGS OF PREY

Chasing small animals is in the blood of many dogs, perhaps most; they think that this is a fun recreational activity (although some are more likely to bring you an undesirable "gift" as a result of the hunt). The good old "Leave it" command works to deter your dog from taking off in pursuit of "prey," but only if taught with the dog on leash for control. The same applies for deterring a dog from chasing cars or bicycles.

The body language of an aggressive dog about to attack is clear. The dog will have a hard, steady stare. He will try to look as big as possible by standing stiff-legged, pushing out his chest, keeping his ears up and holding his tail up and steady. The hackles on his back will rise so that a ridge of hairs stands up. This posture may include the curled lip, snarl and/or growl, or he may be silent. He looks, and definitely is, very dangerous.

This dominant posture is seen in dogs that are territorially aggressive. Deliverymen are constant victims of serious bites from such dogs. Territorial aggression is the reason you should never, ever try to train a puppy to be a watchdog. It can escalate into this type of behavior over which you will have no control. All forms of aggression must be taken seriously and dealt with immediately. If signs of aggressive behavior continue, or grow worse, or if you are at all unsure about how to deal with your dog's behavior, get the help of a professional.

Uncontrolled aggression, sometimes called "irritable aggression," is not something for the pet owner to try to solve. If you cannot solve your dog's dangerous behavior with professional help, and you (quite rightly) do not wish to keep a canine time-bomb in your home, you will have some important decisions to make. Aggressive dogs often cannot be rehomed successfully, as they are dangerous and unreliable in their behavior. An aggressive dog should be dealt with only by someone who knows exactly the situation that he is getting into and has the experience, dedication and ideal living environment to attempt rehabilitating the dog, which may not even be possible. In these cases, the dog ends up having to be humanely put down. Making a decision about euthanasia is not an easy undertaking for anyone, for any reason, but you cannot pass on to another home a dog that you know could cause harm.

A puppy that persists with nuisance behaviors requires unflagging consistency from his owner until he gets the idea that he is acting inappropriately.

A milder form of aggression is the dog's guarding anything that he perceives to be his—his food dish, his toys, his bed and/or his crate. This can be prevented if you take firm control from the start. The young puppy can and should be taught that his leader will share, but that certain rules apply. Guarding is mild aggression only in the beginning stages, and it will

GET A WHIFF OF HIM!

Dogs sniff each others' rears as their way of saying "Hi" as well as to find out who the other dog is and how he's doing. That's normal behavior between canines, but it can, annoyingly, extend to people. The command for all unwanted sniffing is "Leave it!" Give the command in a no-nonsense voice and move on.

A dog's anticipation of his owner's arrival does not necessarily signal separation anxiety, just that he's happy to see the person he loves.

worsen and become dangerous if you let it.

Don't try to snatch anything away from your puppy. Bargain for the item in question so that you can positively reinforce him when he gives it up. Punishment only results in worsening any aggressive behavior.

Many dogs extend their guarding impulse toward items they've stolen. The dog figures, "If I have it, it's mine!" (Some ill-behaved kids have similar tendencies.) An angry confrontation will only increase the dog's aggression. (Have you ever watched a child have a tantrum?) Try a simple distraction first, such as tossing a toy or picking up his leash for a walk. If that doesn't work, the best way to handle the situation is with basic obedience. Show the dog a treat, followed by calm, almost slow-motion commands: "Come. Sit. Drop it. Good dog," and then hand over the cheese! That's one example of positive-reinforcement training.

Children can be bitten when they try to retrieve a stolen shoe or toy, so they need to know how to handle the dog or to let an adult do it. They may also be bitten as they run away from a dog, in either fear or play. The dog sees the child's running as reason for pursuit, and even a friendly young puppy will nip at the heels of a runaway. Teach the kids not to run away from a strange dog and when to stop overly exciting play with their own puppy.

Fear biting is yet another aggressive behavior. A fear biter gives many warning signals. The dog leans away from the approaching person (sometimes hiding behind his owner) with his ears and tail down, but not in submission. He may even shiver.

His hackles are raised, his lips curled. When the person steps into the dog's "flight zone" (a circle of 1 to 3 feet surrounding the dog), he attacks. Because of the fear factor, he performs a rapid attack-and-retreat. Because it is directed at a person, vets are often the victims of this form of aggression. It is frightening, but discovering and eliminating the cause of the fright will help overcome the dog's need to bite. Early socialization again plays a strong role in the prevention of this behavior. Again, if you can't cope with it, get the help of an expert.

SEPARATION ANXIETY

Any behaviorist will tell you that separation anxiety is the most common problem about which pet owners complain. It is also one of the easiest to prevent. Unfortunately, a behaviorist usually is not consulted until the dog is a stressed-out, neurotic mess. At that stage, it is indeed a problem that requires the help of a professional.

Training the puppy to the fact that people in the house come and go is essential in order to avoid this anxiety. Leaving the puppy in his crate or a confined area while family members go in and out, and stay out for longer and longer periods of time, is the basic way to desensitize the pup to the family's frequent departures. If you are at home most of every day, make it a point to go out for at least an hour or two whenever possible.

How you leave is vital to the dog's reaction. Your dog is no fool. He knows the difference between sweats and business suits, jeans and dresses. He sees you pat your pocket to check for your wallet, open your briefcase, check that you have your cell phone or pick up the car keys. He knows from the hurry of the kids

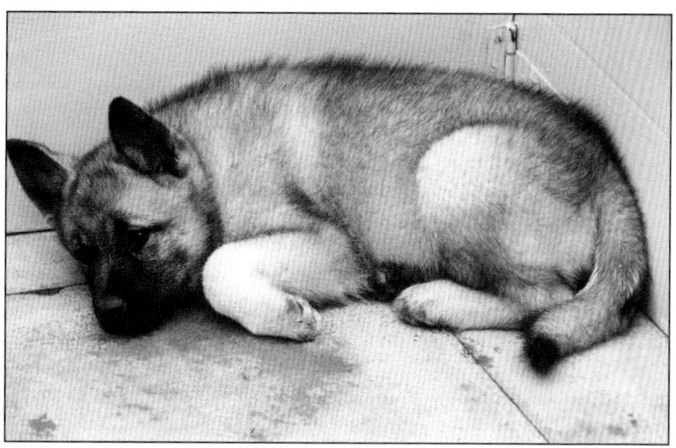

Is your Elkhound lost without you? Fortunately, a dog can be desensitized to his owner's comings and goings so that he will feel confident and comfortable when left alone.

> **DOMINANCE**
>
> Dogs are born with dominance skills, meaning that they can be quite clever in trying to get their way. The "follow-me" trot to the cookie jar is an example. The toy dropped in your lap says "Play with me." The leash delivered to you along with an excited look means "Take me for a walk." These are all good-natured dominant behaviors. Ask your dog to sit before agreeing to his request and you'll remain "top dog."

Elkhounds are intelligent dogs that respond to fair, consistent treatment and methods based on positive reinforcement.

in the morning that they're off to school until afternoon. Lipstick? Aftershave lotion? Lunch boxes? Every move you make registers in his sensory perception and memory. Your puppy knows more about your departures than you might expect. You can't get away with a thing!

Before you got dressed, you checked the dog's water bowl and his supply of long-lasting chew toys, and turned the radio on low. You will leave him in what he considers his "safe" area, not with total freedom of the house. If you've invested in child safety gates, you can be reasonably sure that he'll remain in the designated area. Don't give him access to a window where he can watch you leave the house. If you're leaving for an hour or two, just put him into his crate with a safe toy.

Now comes the test! You are ready to walk out the door. Do not give your Norwegian Elkhound a big hug and a fond farewell. Do not drag out a long goodbye. Those are the very things that jump-start separation anxiety. Toss a biscuit into the dog's area, call out "So long, pooch" and close the door. You're gone. The chances are that the dog may bark a couple of times, or maybe whine once or twice, and then settle down to enjoy his biscuit and take a lovely nap, especially if you took him for a nice long walk before leaving. As he grows up, the barks and whines will stop because it's an old routine, so why should he make the effort?

LOOK AT ME WHEN I SPEAK TO YOU

Your dog considers direct eye contact as a sign of dominance. A shy dog will avoid looking at you; a dominant dog will try to stare you down. What you want is for your dog to pay attention when you speak, and that doesn't necessarily involve direct eye contact. In dealing with a problem dog, avert your gaze momentarily, return to face the dog and give an immediate down command. Show him that you're the boss.

When you first brought home the puppy, the come-and-go routine was intermittent and constant. He was put into his crate with a tiny treat. You left (silently) and returned in 3 minutes, then 5, then 10, then 15, then half an hour, until finally you could leave without a problem and be gone for 2 or 3 hours. If, at any time in the future, there's a "separation" problem, refresh his memory by going back to that basic training.

Now comes the next most important part—your return. Do not make a big production of coming home. "Hi, poochie" is as grand a greeting as he needs. When you've taken off your hat and coat, tossed your briefcase on the hall table and glanced at the mail, and the dog has settled down from the excitement of seeing you "in person" from his confined area, then go and give him a warm, friendly greeting. A potty trip is needed and a walk would be appreciated, since he's been such a good dog.

CHEWING

All puppies chew. All dogs chew. This is a fact of life for canines, and sometimes you may think it's what your dog does best! Norwegian Elkhounds are chewers, especially when bored. Elkhounds do bore easily, so you must have an array of interesting toys plus make sure that your dog gets plenty of activity and exercise.

A pup starts chewing when his first set of teeth erupts and continues throughout the teething period. Chewing gives the pup relief from itchy gums and incoming teeth and, from that time on, he gets great satisfaction out of this normal, somewhat idle, canine activity. Providing safe chew toys is the best way to direct this behavior in an appropriate manner. Chew toys are available in all sizes, textures and flavors, but you must monitor the wear-and-tear inflicted on your pup's toys to be sure that the

Chewing is a natural (and favorite) activity for most dogs. Both puppies and adult dogs do their share of chewing and should be provided with safe, healthy chew devices.

Elkhounds are talented diggers; thus, extra attention needs to be paid to making your yard secure and truly escape-proof.

ones you've chosen are safe and remain in good condition.

Puppies cannot distinguish between a rawhide toy and a nice leather shoe or wallet. It's up to you to keep your possessions away from the dog and to keep your eye on the dog. There's a form of destruction caused by chewing that is not the dog's fault. Let's say you allow him on the sofa. One day he takes a rawhide bone up on the sofa and, in the course of chewing on the bone, takes up a bit of fabric. He continues to chew. Disaster! Now you've learned the lesson: Dogs with chew toys have to be either kept off furniture and carpets, carefully supervised or put into their confined areas for chew time.

The wooden legs of furniture are favorite objects for chewing. The first time, tell the dog "Leave it!" (or "No!") and offer him a chew toy as a substitute. But your clever dog may be hiding under the chair and doing some silent destruction, which you may not notice until it's too late. In this case, it's time to try one of the foul-tasting products, made specifically to prevent destructive chewing, that is sprayed on the objects of your dog's chewing attention. These products also work to keep the dog away from plants, trash, etc. It's even a good way to stop the dog from "mouthing" or chewing on your hands or the leg of your pants. (Be sure to wash your hands after the mouthing lesson!) A little spray goes a long way.

DIGGING

Digging is another natural and normal doggy behavior. Digging behavior has long-established roots in dogs, as wild canines would dig to bury whatever food they could save for later to eat. (And you thought *we* invented the doggie bag!) Thus, burying bones or toys is a primary cause for today's dogs to dig. Dogs also dig to get at interesting little underground creatures like moles and mice. In the summer, they dig to get down to cool earth. In winter, they dig to get beneath the cold surface to warmer earth.

The solution to the last two is easy. In the summer, provide a bed that's up off the ground and placed in a shaded area. In winter, the dog should either be indoors to sleep or given an adequate insulated doghouse outdoors. To understand how natural and normal this is, you have only to consider the Nordic breeds, like your Elkhound, who instinctively dig beds for themselves in the snow. It's the nesting instinct. How often have you seen your dog go round and round in circles, pawing at his blanket or bedding before flopping down to sleep?

Domesticated dogs also dig to escape, and that's a lot more dangerous than it is destructive.

THE MACHO DOG

The Venus/Mars differences are found in dogs, too. Males have distinct behaviors that, while seemingly sex-related, are more closely connected to the role of the male as leader. Marking territory by urinating on it is one means that male dogs use to establish their presence. Doing so merely says, "I've been here." Small dogs often attempt to lift their legs higher on the tree than the previous male. While this is natural behavior outdoors on items like telephone poles, fence posts, fire hydrants and most other upright objects, marking indoors is totally unacceptable. Treat it as you would a house-training accident and clean thoroughly to eradicate the scent. Another behavior often seen in the macho male, mounting is a dominance display. Neutering the dog before six months of age helps to deter this behavior. You can discourage him from mounting by catching the dog as he's about to mount you, stepping quickly aside and saying "Off!"

The Elkhound is a vocal (and loud!) breed that will look after his family's property and sound the alarm at most anything unfamiliar.

A dog that digs under the fence is the one that is hit by a car or becomes lost. A good fence to protect an Elkhound should be set 10 to 12 inches below ground level, and every fence needs to be routinely checked for even the smallest openings that can become possible escape routes.

Catching your dog in the act of digging is the easiest way to stop it because your dog will make the "one-plus-one" connection, but digging is too often a solitary occupation, something the lonely dog does out of boredom. Catch your young puppy in the act and put a stop to it before you have a yard full of craters. It is more difficult to stop if your dog sees you gardening. If you can dig, why can't he? Because you say so, that's why! The propensity for an Elkhound to dig will vary among individuals, but in general this is a breed that likes to use its paws.

BARKING

Here's a big, noisy problem! Telling a dog he must never bark is like telling a child not to speak! Consider how confusing it must be to your dog that you are using your voice (which is your form of barking) to teach him when to bark and when not to! That is precisely the reason not to "bark back" when the dog's barking is annoying you (or your neighbors). Try to understand the scenario from the dog's viewpoint. He barks. You bark. He barks again, you bark again. This "conversation"can go on forever!

The Norwegian Elkhound is a vocal breed. He is very alert and has a loud bark, and he will use it whenever he hears an unexpected noise or suspects that an intruder is approaching. As an owner, you must choose how to react to your Elkhound's vocalizations. For example, the first time your adorable little puppy said "Yip" or "Yap, you were ecstatic. His first word! You smiled, you told him how smart he was—and you allowed him to do it. So there's that one-plus-one thing again, because he will understand by your happy reaction that "Mr. Alpha loves it when I talk." Ignore his barking in the beginning, and allow it, but don't encourage barking during play. Instead, use the "put a toy in it" method to tone it down. Add a very soft "Quiet" as you hand off the toy. If the barking continues, stand up straight, fold your arms and turn your back on the dog. If he barks, you won't play, and you should follow the same rule for all undesirable behavior during play.

Dogs bark in reaction to sounds and sights. Another dog's bark, a person passing by or even just rustling leaves can set off a barker. If someone coming up your driveway or to your door provokes a barking frenzy, use the saturation method to stop it. Have several friends come and go every three or four minutes over as long a period of time as they can spare (it could take a couple of hours). Attach about a foot of rope to the dog's collar and have very small treats handy. Each time a car pulls up or a person approaches, let the dog bark once (grab the rope if you need to physically restrain him), say "Okay, good dog," give him a treat and make him sit. "Okay" is the release command. It lets the dog know that he has alerted you and tells him that you are now in charge. That person leaves and the next arrives, and so on and so on until everyone—especially the dog—is bored and the barking has stopped. Don't forget to

When food is around, you can be sure the dog will figure out a way to get it. The best way to prevent food stealing is to keep all theft-worthy tidbits where the dog truly cannot get to them.

STORM WARNING

Dogs sense approaching storms by barometric pressure changes. Many dogs do not like storms and head for cover under the bed, in a corner, in a closet, under a table, wherever they feel safe. To desensitize your dog to storms and to show him that he has nothing to fear, buy an audiotape of thunderstorm sounds. Set it so that you can barely hear it and sit in a closed room, where you'll read the paper while your dog listens to his new "storm" toy. Turn it off after a few fearless minutes. Repeat, increasing the sound level only as the dog tolerates it.

thank your friends. Your neighbors, by the way, may be more than willing to assist you in this parlor game if it means a quiet dog on the block.

Excessive barking outdoors is more difficult to keep in check because, when it happens, he is outside and you are probably inside. A few warning barks are fine, but use the same method to tell him when enough is enough. You will have to stay outside with him for that bit of training.

There is one more kind of vocalizing, which is called "idiot barking" (from idiopathic, meaning of unknown cause). It is usually rhythmic or a timed series of barks. Put a stop to it immediately by calling the dog to come. This form of barking can drive neighbors crazy and commonly occurs when a dog is left outside for long periods of time. He is completely and thoroughly bored! A change of scenery may help, such as relocating him to a room indoors when he is used to being outside. A few new toys or different dog biscuits might be the solution. If he is left alone while you are at work and no one can get home during the day, a noontime walk with a local dog-sitter would be the perfect solution.

FOOD-RELATED PROBLEMS

We're not talking about eating, diets or nutrition here, we're talking about bad habits. Face it. All dogs are beggars. Food is the motivation for everything we want our dogs to do and, when you combine that with their innate ability to "con" us in order to get their way, it's a wonder there aren't far more obese dogs in the world.

Who can resist the bleeding-heart look that says "I'm starving," or the paw that gently pats your knee and gives you a knowing look, or the whining "please" or even the total body language of a perfect sit beneath the cookie jar. No one who professes to love his dog can turn down the pleas of his clever canine's performances every time. One thing is for sure, though: definitely do not allow begging at the table. Family meals do not include your dog.

Control your dog's begging habit by making your dog work

FOUR ON THE FLOOR

You must discourage your dog from jumping up to get attention or for any other reason. To do so, turn away from the dog as he jumps up, not allowing him to make physical contact with you, as any contact serves as a reward to him. "Four on the floor" requires praise. Once the dog sits on command, prevent him from attempting to jump again by asking him to sit-stay before petting him. Back away if he breaks the sit.

for his rewards. Ignore his begging when you can. Utilize the obedience commands you've taught your dog. Use "Off" for the pawing. A sit or even a long down will interrupt the whining. His reward in these situations is definitely not a treat! Casual verbal praise is enough. Be sure that all members of the family follow the same rules.

There is a different type of begging that does demand your immediate response and that is the appeal to be let (or taken) outside! Usually that is a quick paw or small whine to get your attention, followed by a race to the door. This type of begging needs your quick attention and approval. Of course, a really smart dog will soon figure out how to cut you off at the pass and direct you to that cookie jar on your way to the door! Some dogs are always one step ahead of us.

The only way to teach a dog to beg is to give in to his begging! Feeding your dog under the dinner table or throwing him scraps as you're preparing food are no-no's.

STOP, THIEF!

The easiest way to prevent a dog from stealing food is to stop this behavior before it starts by never leaving food out where he can reach it. However, if it is too late, and your dog has already made a steal, you must stop your furry felon from becoming a repeat offender. Once Sneaky Pete has successfully stolen food, place a bit of food where he can reach it. Place an empty soda can with some pebbles in it on top of the food. Leave the room and watch what happens. As the dog grabs the tasty morsel, the can comes with it. The noise of the tumbling pebble-filled can makes its own correction, and you don't have to say a word.

INDEX

*Page numbers in **boldface** indicate illustrations.*

My Norwegian Elkhound

PUT YOUR PUPPY'S FIRST PICTURE HERE

Dog's Name ___________________________

Date ______________ Photographer ______________________